Writing from Within Intro

Arlen Gargagliano & Curtis Kelly

Teacher's Manual

CAMBRIDGE
UNIVERSITY PRESS

PUBLISHED BY THE PRESS SYNDICATE OF THE UNIVERSITY OF CAMBRIDGE

The Pitt Building, Trumpington Street, Cambridge, United Kingdom

CAMBRIDGE UNIVERSITY PRESS

The Edinburgh Building, Cambridge CB2 2RU, UK

40 West 20th Street, New York, NY 10011-4211, USA

477 Williamstown Road, Port Melbourne, VIC 3207, Australia

Ruiz de Alarcón 13, 28014 Madrid, Spain

Nautica Building, The Water Club, Beach Road, Granger Bay, Cape Town 8005, South Africa

http://www.cambridge.org

© Cambridge University Press 2005

First published 2005

Printed in Hong Kong, China

Typeface New Century Schoolbook   *System* Quark 4.1

A catalog record for this book is available from the British Library

ISBN 0 521 60626 8   Student's Book
ISBN 0 521 60625 X   Teacher's Manual

Book design: Adventure House, NYC

Layout services: NK Graphics, Keene, New Hampshire

Contents

Plan of the book

Writing	Editing	Option
☐ writing a letter of introduction	☐ connecting sentences	☐ writing addresses and signatures
☐ writing about a special place	☐ prepositional phrases	☐ making a tourist guidebook
☐ writing about an ideal partner	☐ parallel structure	☐ creating dating game characters
☐ writing about a favorite photo	☐ present or past?	☐ making a picture time line
☐ writing about a personal seal	☐ commas with *because*	☐ making a group flag
☐ writing a notice and paragraph for a class party	☐ *so that* and *to*	☐ designing a party poster
☐ writing a thank-you letter	☐ *before* and *after*	☐ writing a letter to a company
☐ writing a movie review	☐ pronouns	☐ producing a movie
☐ writing about a friend	☐ combining sentences with *so*	☐ writing a magazine article
☐ writing about a superhero power	☐ expressing wishes II	☐ writing a comic book story
☐ writing an advertisement	☐ persuasive language	☐ advertising for a class flea market
☐ writing about something you regret	☐ word choice	☐ designing a card

For a student who has never written more than a single sentence at a time, drafting a whole paragraph, even a short one, is a daunting challenge. Yet by writing even short texts, a whole new avenue for communication opens up. There are things students will write that they would never say, and writing offers them the potential to go deeply into their inner worlds. We, as authors, believe that all language learners, even low-level learners, possess a need to express themselves and share what is meaningful to them.

This book was written for such learners. Our goal was to create activities that not only allow them to succeed at writing English, but also allow them to express personal, meaningful, and sometimes fanciful facets of their lives. Low-level learners, too, have inner worlds. In addition, we have tried to create activities that pull our learners into writing rather than push them.

Writing from Within Intro covers a spectrum of educational objectives. Students are taught how to write sentences, generate and organize content, structure and sequence this content into paragraphs, review and edit what they have written, and finally, how to respond to what others have written. We see writing as a balanced combination of language, expository, and self-revelation skills.

Like its predecessor, *Writing from Within,* the focus of each unit is a writing assignment. Some assignments are introspective: For example, learners are asked to reflect on something they are thankful for. Others are more conventional but task-based: Learners are asked to write movie reviews and advertisements. In this way, humanistic writing assignments are balanced with task-based writing assignments to provide a broad range of writing experiences. In addition, each unit ends with an optional expansion activity that gives learners the opportunity to apply their new skills to a different task.

At the center of each unit is a writing assignment. Five of the lessons in each unit are prewriting activities that should be completed before the first draft is written. Prewriting activities include generating and organizing information, and learning basic language structures. Expository skills, such as how to write topic and supporting sentences, are also taught. Two lessons follow the writing assignment: The editing lesson teaches learners to enrich their writing by making stylistic choices. The feedback lesson gives learners the opportunity to respond to their classmates' writing. Each unit takes 3–5 hours of class time to complete, and although the syllabus is developmental, it is not necessary to do each unit in order.

The Teacher's Manual is designed to give specific ideas on using the Student's Book and tips for adapting it to suit your classroom. We suggest you take the time to familiarize yourself with the style and themes of the Student's Book before you begin teaching.

Writing is a skill. We tell our students that learning to write is like learning to play a musical instrument: the more they practice, the better they will be. *Writing from Within Intro* is designed to demonstrate to learners that they have the knowledge and ability within to develop this skill. We hope they will enjoy this text, and we look forward to hearing your comments.

Arlen Gargagliano
Curtis Kelly

How should I use the Teacher's Manual?

The Teacher's Manual is designed to give you practical guidelines for teaching *Writing from Within Intro*. Each unit in the Teacher's Manual is about seven pages long. It is divided into four sections: 1) a short **Overview** that tells you what the students will do and learn; 2) a Table of contents with the lesson focus and the expected times to complete each lesson; 3) a list of **Key points** – things to keep in mind; and 4) detailed Instructions for each lesson, an Answer Key, and Optional Activities to provide further practice.

Whether you are a new or experienced teacher, we hope that this material will help guide your lessons. You know your students best; you should adapt the lessons based on the size, background, and length of your classes. Our advice is to follow the Teacher's Manual closely for the first few units until you feel comfortable with the book, and then use it when you need suggestions, answers, and additional activities.

What is the basic organization of a unit in the Student's Book?

Prewriting
Brainstorming: The writing topic is introduced and writing ideas are generated.

Analyzing sentences: Students read a short paragraph for meaning and notice features of key sentence types.

Learning about organization: Students learn expository organizational skills and how to support the ideas in their writing.

Writing
Model and assignment: Students analyze a model and receive instructions for writing their paragraphs.

Postwriting
Journal: Students develop writing fluency with freer individual practice.

Editing: Students focus on language and style points they can use to improve their writing.

Giving feedback: Students exchange paragraphs with other students for review and feedback.

Option: The optional writing activity builds on the students' newly gained skills by giving them a related writing activity that is both enjoyable and practical.

What is the purpose of the peer feedback lesson?

Peer feedback is not the same as peer correction. When students read their classmates' papers, they are exposed to meaningful models for their own writing, and they develop their ability to analyze and evaluate writing. Writers get feedback from their peers to let them know how successfully they communicated their ideas. Since the peer feedback puts the focus on the message rather than the performance, each writer is ensured a real audience. This lesson also makes the textbook easier to use in large classes, since it takes some of the burden of giving feedback off the teacher.

What are the optional writing activities at the end of each unit?

The final lesson in each unit is an optional second writing assignment. It involves extending the language and writing skills learned in the unit to an enjoyable real-world task such as making a card, creating a movie plot, or designing a poster. Students may incorporate speaking and group project work into their writing activities. Many of the activities also allow visually-oriented students to add elements of graphic design such as illustration and layout to their writing. These visual elements are also an important part of written communication. For students with weaker writing skills, working with visuals increases their ability to communicate and allows them to succeed in one part of a task they might otherwise have difficulty with.

How are grammar and vocabulary handled in the lessons?

Grammar is not taught directly in this writing course. It is taught indirectly through exercises in which students are exposed to and asked to notice key grammatical forms, manipulate them, and then incorporate them into their writing. Vocabulary appropriate for the unit's main writing assignment is taught in the same way.

Can I skip certain units or lessons?

The units gradually increase in difficulty, and features from one unit are recycled in subsequent units, but it is still possible to skip units or do them in a different order. If you do not have time in your course to complete all of the units, choose the ones your students will be most interested in.

Lessons in individual units can also be skipped if necessary. The *Key points* section of the Teacher's Manual indicates the minimum set of lessons that must be completed in order to do the main writing assignment in Lesson 6.

How do I deal with mixed levels of students?

Deciding to put similar or mixed level students together in a group depends on a number of factors, including learning styles, culture, and classroom dynamics. Experiment with grouping students in different ways.

Keep in mind that it is not necessary for every student to answer every question for learning to occur, and that the "compare answers with a partner" exercise at the end of many lessons exists, in part, to help alleviate this problem. Pairing weaker students with better ones, in a sort of mentorship, can be effective in helping both learn.

A greater problem might exist when students finish an activity before the others and are left with nothing to do. Optional expansion activities in this Teacher's Manual and journal assignments are available to give such students additional challenges.

What is the purpose of the journal?

The journal writing task is an option for teachers who want their students to do additional writing or for use in classes where more fluent students finish the writing assignment sooner than the rest.

The exercises in the Student's Book guide students to write accurate sentences. The journal provides the opportunity for students to write more freely and develop writing fluency. It also allows stronger and weaker level students to write at their own level.

The journal is a place where you can offer individual encouragement. We suggest you write short notes similar to the ones that students write to each other in Lesson 8. You can start with, "Dear _____ , Thank you for telling me about _____ ." Share some of your own information, ask questions, or simply make brief comments. To encourage fluency, don't correct grammar directly, but respond to students' ideas; grading should be based on effort. Since students may write personal or sensitive information in their journals, make sure they know who will be reading them (just you? other students?). Do not let others read students' journals without their knowledge or permission.

How often should I give homework?

This depends entirely on how your class is scheduled and the type of students you are teaching. The book is set up so that most of the activities can be done as homework. We suggest that you give regular homework assignments so that students practice their writing skills outside as well as inside of class.

How should I evaluate student writing?

This depends on your particular goals, as well as the grading standards set by your school. If making your students *feel successful* at writing is your main goal,

then evaluate students according to completion, effort, and how other readers rate the writing. If *communicative competence* is your main goal, pay more attention to content, how well students organize their papers, and language use. If *correct English* is your goal, then spend more time assessing accuracy and have students revise their papers. Note that although many teachers set accuracy as the main goal and engage in extensive error correction, we do not recommend it.

In addition to writing comments on students' papers, we recommend that you meet with your students to discuss their writing, language goals, and ways they can improve.

You can choose whether to have your students revise their papers or not. If you do have them submit revisions, have them attach the original as well. You might ask them to keep a portfolio of all their work. You could give one grade for the original writing and another for the revision, so that they have the opportunity to improve their grade. You could also give one grade for content and organization and another for language use. The most important point to consider in grading papers is that students be encouraged.

Writing from Within Intro

Teacher's Manual

Preview

Overview

This unit introduces students to the concept and key parts of a paragraph, as well as to the philosophy of *Writing from Within Intro*.

▪ Read the instructions for the first exercise aloud.

▪ Have students work with a partner to answer the question.

▪ Call on a student to give the answer.

▪ Note that students can do the exercise without reading the paragraphs.

> **Answer**
> Example b uses paragraphs.

▪ Read the information under *A paragraph has a special shape* aloud. Point out each feature mentioned in the example paragraphs in b above.

▪ Read the explanation under *A paragraph is usually between two and seven sentences long* aloud.

▪ Have students answer the question about paragraph length individually.

▪ Call on a student to give the answer.

> **Answer**
> The first paragraph in example b is four sentences long.

▪ Read the information under *A paragraph is about one main idea* aloud.

▪ Call on students to read the paragraph aloud, sentence by sentence. Explain vocabulary as necessary.

▪ Have students answer the questions about the topics of the paragraphs individually.

▪ Call on a student to give the answers.

> **Answers**
> The topic of the first paragraph in example b is *last year's experiences*.
>
> The topic of the second paragraph in example b is *getting married*.

▪ Have students read the letter individually.

▪ Call on students to read the letter aloud, sentence by sentence. Explain vocabulary as necessary.

> **Optional activity**
>
> ### My goal
> Write the sentence My goal in this class is to
> _____ . on the board. Ask students to copy the sentence and complete it. Then call on individual students to read their goals aloud. Though of course their goal is to learn to write in English, try to elicit exact reasons (e.g., for work, for my education, for my family, etc.).

Unit **1** *Who am I?*

Overview

This first unit familiarizes students with the basic lessons used in each unit in this book. Students are introduced to the writing process and learn to brainstorm, write a paragraph, and check and revise their work.

The first five lessons introduce students to the prewriting activities of brainstorming and organizing ideas. The central writing assignment of the unit, an e-mail letter of introduction, is presented in Lesson 6. The postwriting lessons, Lessons 7 and 8, include combining sentences with *and* and *but* and a peer feedback lesson where students read and comment on classmates' paragraphs. The *Option: Just for fun* lesson gives students practice writing their addresses and handwritten and e-mail signatures.

	Lesson	Focus	Estimated Time
1	What is brainstorming?	Brainstorming	20–30 minutes
2	Meet Luigi	Analyzing sentences	15–25 minutes
3	Letters of introduction	Learning about organization	20–30 minutes
4	Topics	Learning about organization	20–30 minutes
5	Information interview	Prewriting	20–30 minutes
6	My letter of introduction	Writing	30–40 minutes
7	Connecting sentences	Editing	20–30 minutes
8	What do you think?	Giving feedback	20–30 minutes
	Addresses	Option: Just for fun	15–25 minutes

Key points

➤ The activities in this unit help students learn more about their classmates, so they'll be comfortable working together throughout the course.

➤ Take time to explain the purpose of each lesson as you go along, so students will know how to handle similar lessons in the following units.

➤ Useful language for this unit includes the simple present tense to give general information.

➤ Time can be reduced if some parts of the lessons are assigned as homework activities and class time is used for checking the answers.

➤ Sections can be skipped. A minimal set of lessons might include 1, 2, 3, 4, and 6.

Lesson 1 What is brainstorming?

pages 4–5

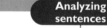

- On the board, draw a brain and a storm cloud raining ideas down on the brain.
- Tell students that "to brainstorm" means "to write new ideas quickly."
- Read the explanation at the top of page 4.
- To give an example, say, *Let's brainstorm together*. Write *vacation* on the board. Ask, *What does the word "vacation" make you think of?*
- Write a few examples on the board, such as *relaxation, beach, more sleep,* and *I like seeing friends.* Call on students for more examples and write them on the board.
- Tell students that the point of brainstorming is to collect a lot of ideas to work with. They can decide not to use some ideas later.

1

- Call on students to read the ideas from Luigi's brainstorming chart aloud. Explain vocabulary as necessary.

2

- Read the instructions for Exercise 2 aloud.
- Ask students to tell you what they see in the pictures. Provide vocabulary as necessary.
- Have students work individually to identify Luigi, and then compare answers with a partner. Have students explain how they knew the other pictures were not Luigi.
- Call on a pair to give the answer.

> **Answer**
> **2.** c

3

- Read the instructions for Exercise 3 aloud.
- Have students brainstorm about themselves. Set a time limit of five minutes.
- Ask students not to use a dictionary at this point, to help them think in English instead of translating.
- Tell students they can fill in the blanks with any kind of information about themselves, not just the same information Luigi wrote.

4

- Have students introduce themselves to a classmate using the information they wrote in Exercise 3.

Optional activity

Party
Tell students to imagine they are at a party. Have students stand and walk around the room to introduce themselves and talk to as many classmates as possible. Set a time limit of ten minutes. Then ask students what they learned about each other by calling on individuals.

Lesson 2 Meet Luigi

page 6

Analyzing sentences

- Tell students they will read an example of a letter of introduction and tell them to notice the language used.

1

- Read the instruction at the top of page 6.
- Have students read the paragraph individually.
- Call on students to read the paragraph aloud, sentence by sentence. Explain vocabulary as necessary.
- Point out that this paragraph was written by Luigi, whose brainstorming chart they read in Lesson 1.

- Read the instruction for Exercise 1a and the six topics under the pictures aloud. Explain vocabulary as necessary. Tell students that there is one sentence in the paragraph for each topic.
- Have students complete the exercise individually.
- Read the instructions for 1b aloud.
- Write sentence 2 from the paragraph in Exercise 1 on the board. Point out the comma between the two clauses and the period at the end.
- Have students complete 1b individually.
- Ask students to raise their hands or nod at you when they have finished.

2

- Have students compare answers with a partner.
- Go over answers as a whole class.

> **Answers**
> **I. a.** his job: 4
> his interests: 6
> his name: 1
> his age and nationality: 2
> his home: 3
> his future plans: 5
>
> **b.** I am Spanish, and I am 16 years old.

Optional activity

Substitution game
Write the paragraph from page 6 on the board with the following words underlined:

My name is <u>Luigi</u>. I am <u>Italian</u>, and I am <u>32</u> years old. I live in a <u>small apartment</u> in <u>Rome</u>. I work in a <u>clothing store</u>. Some day I want to be <u>the manager</u>. <u>Tennis</u> is my favorite <u>sport</u>, but I like <u>baseball</u>, too.

Students take turns reading the sentences aloud, substituting different words for the underlined ones.

Lesson 3	**Letters of introduction**

Learning about organization

page 7

- Tell students they will learn how to begin and end an e-mail letter of introduction.
- Read the information at the top of page 7 aloud.

I

- Read the instructions for Exercise 1 aloud.
- Tell students to look at Maria's e-mail. Read the e-mail aloud and point out how each part of her e-mail corresponds to the topics *name*, *age*, *nationality*, and *gender*.
- Have students complete a–c individually.
- Check answers by calling on some students to write their sentences on the board. While they are writing, walk around the classroom to check other students' sentences.

> **Answers**
> **I.** Answers will vary. Possible answers:
>
> **a.** My name is Min Ho.
>
> **b.** I am 19 years old.
>
> **c.** I am a Korean man.

2

- Read the instructions for Exercise 2 aloud.
- Call on a student to read the phrases in the Word Files aloud. Point out that greetings come at the beginning of a letter and closings come at the end, just before the writer's name.
- Point out that *Hello!* and *Hi there,* are informal greetings used between friends and family members.

- Have students work individually to complete Exercise 2.

3

- Read the instruction for Exercise 3 aloud.
- Have students complete the exercise individually.
- You may want to take additional class time to correct errors on individual letters, or you can have students copy their letters onto a separate sheet of paper to turn in for correction.
- You may also have volunteers write their e-mail excerpts on the board. Go over them with the whole class.

> **Answer**
> **2.** Answers will vary. Possible answer:
>
> Dear Jun Hee,
>
> My name is Kazu. I am 20 years old. I am a Japanese man.
>
> Best wishes,
> Kazu

Optional activity

Additional greetings and closings
Have students find some more greetings and closings. They can use their own knowledge, look in books or on the Internet, or ask native speakers. They should also find out whether the greetings and closings are formal or informal.

page 8

Learning about organization

- Tell students they will learn what topics to write about in a letter of introduction.

I

- Have a student read the top of page 8, including the topics.
- Read the instructions for Exercise 1 aloud.
- Read 1a aloud. Point out that the topic comes from the list at the top of page 8.
- Call on a student to read the example sentence. Tell students to write sentences about themselves and their lives.
- Have students complete b–h individually. Walk around the classroom, helping students as necessary.
- Elicit responses from the class.

Answers

I. Sentences will vary. Possible answers:

   a. school: I go to a university.

   b. interests: I go snowboarding in my free time.

   c. future plans: I want to be an engineer.

   d. your job: I don't have a job.

   e. pets: I have two birds.

   f. friends: My best friend lives near me.

   g. likes and dislikes: I don't like hot weather.

   h. family: I live with my parents and my grandmother.

Optional activity

Who is it?

Have students write sentences about the topics in Exercise 1 on small pieces of paper and put them into a bag. Mix them up and have each student draw one out. Students read the sentence aloud and guess who wrote it. Turn this into a game by having students stand up and ask questions to discover the writer (e.g., Are you a junior college student?).

page 9

Prewriting

- Tell students they will ask and answer questions with a partner to get more information about the topics from Lesson 4.

I

- Read the instructions for Exercise 1 aloud.
- Call on four pairs of students to read the dialogues.
- Have students work with a partner to complete the exercise.
- If students need more practice, have them change partners and repeat the exercise.
- Walk around the classroom, helping students as necessary.

2

- Read the instructions for Exercise 2 aloud.
- Have a student read the examples.
- Have students complete the exercise individually.
- Encourage students to write more than one additional sentence per topic if they can.
- Call on students to read their sentences aloud or write them on the board. You may also have students read their sentences in groups and choose the most interesting answers to share with the rest of the class.

Answers

2. Answers will vary. Possible answers:

    a. I go to a university. I will graduate in February.

    b. I have two birds. They are parakeets.

    c. I live with my parents and my grandmother. She is 86 years old.

    d. I live in a small town near Yokohama. It is famous for its beaches.

Optional activity

Matching follow-up information

Have students write their "sentences" and "more information" from Exercise 2 on separate slips of paper. Put the students in groups of three and have them combine and shuffle their slips of paper. Have them exchange their set with another group. Students in each group work together to figure out which "more information" goes with which "sentence."

Lesson 6   My letter of introduction

pages 10–11   **Writing**

◾ Tell students that they will write a letter of introduction as the main writing assignment for this unit. They will use the information they brainstormed in previous lessons.

1

◾ Read the instructions for Exercise 1 aloud.

◾ Have students read the letter individually.

◾ Call on students to read the letter aloud.

◾ Have students complete a–e individually or with a partner. Walk around the classroom, helping students as necessary.

◾ Go over answers as a whole class.

Answers

1. a. greeting: Dear Mr. and Mrs. Jones
      closing: Sincerely, Lin

    b. I will be your homestay guest for this summer, so let me tell you about myself.

    c. I am a 24-year-old Taiwanese woman.

    d. her family, her future plans, her home, her interests, her school

    e. Best wishes, Yours truly

2

◾ Read the instruction for Exercise 2 aloud.

◾ Point out to students that they will write a greeting, their sentences from Lesson 5, and a closing with their name.

3

◾ Have students write their letter on lined paper or type it. Have them skip lines so that they can edit their letter more easily and you can correct it more easily.

◾ Have students complete their letter in class or at home.

◾ Students can also e-mail their letter to you and to classmates.

◾ Students who finish early should begin the journal assignment.

In your journal . . .

◾ *If time permits, read the journal entry instructions aloud. Tell students they can answer one or both questions (see notes on page viii for more information on the journal).*

◾ *Have students complete the journal in class or at home.*

▨ Have students take turns reading the information and examples on top of page 12 aloud.

▨ Explain that *and* joins two ideas that are similar and that *but* joins two ideas that are contradictory or unexpected.

1

▨ Read the instructions for Exercise 1 aloud.

▨ Call on students to read the paragraph aloud, sentence by sentence. Explain vocabulary as necessary.

▨ Have students complete the exercise individually or with a partner. Walk around the classroom, helping students as necessary.

> *Answers*
> **1. a.** I am Mexican. I live in the United States.
>
> **b.** I have traveled a lot. I have never been to Canada.
>
> **c.** I love math and science. I want to study biology in college.
>
> **d.** In my free time, I like listening to music. I like singing.
>
> **e.** Please write back to me. Tell me something about yourself.

Optional activity

Analyzing Carlita's letter

Have students work with a partner. Have Student A open the book to page 10. Have Student B open the book to page 12. Tell Student A to read Student B instructions a–d on page 10, substituting Carlita *for* Lin. *Go over answers as a whole class. (Note that Carlita does not give her gender. If necessary, tell the class that she and Julie are women).*

2

▨ Read the instructions for Exercise 2 aloud.

▨ Call on a student to read the example aloud. Point out the comma after *Mexican* and how *but* is used to join the sentences.

▨ Have students complete the exercise individually and then compare answers with a partner.

▨ Check answers by calling on students to write the sentences on the board.

> *Answers*
> **2. a.** I am Mexican, but I live in the United States.
>
> **b.** I have traveled a lot, but I have never been to Canada.
>
> **c.** I love math and science, and I want to study biology in college.
>
> **d.** In my free time, I like listening to music, and I like singing.
>
> **e.** Please write back to me, and tell me something about yourself.

3

▨ Read the instructions for Exercise 3 aloud.

▨ If students want to connect any sentences in their letter of introduction from Lesson 6 with *and* or *but*, give them time to revise their letters or assign it as homework.

▨ Ask for volunteers to write their original sentences and their revisions on the board.

▨ Tell students that they are going to read each other's paragraphs and that they will need a sheet of paper for Exercise 2.

1

▨ Read the instructions for Exercises 1 and a–d aloud.

▨ Have students exchange letters with a partner.

- Have students complete a–d individually. Walk around the classroom, helping students as necessary.
- When they finish, tell students to exchange books and review their partner's answers. They can then go on to Exercise 2.

2
- Read the instructions for Exercise 2 aloud.
- Read or call on a student to read the example letter aloud. Point out the greeting, the closing, the sentence that says what the student liked, and the question.
- Have students write their letter to their partner individually.
- Walk around the classroom, helping students as necessary.

3
- Read the instructions for Exercise 3 aloud.
- Have students exchange their letters with their partner. Give them time to tell their partner the answer to the question in the letter.

- Have students revise their paragraphs based on the comments they receive and other ideas they have. They can complete their revisions either in class or at home.
- Have students turn in their revised paragraphs to you (see notes on page viii about assessing student writing).

Optional activity

Who are we?
Have students add a photo or drawing of themselves to their letters of introduction and display them around the classroom. Consider compiling them into a class newsletter or "yearbook" and distributing a copy to each student.

Option | **Addresses**

Just for fun

page 14

- Tell students they are going to write their addresses in English and practice signing their names and writing e-mail signatures.

1
- Read the instructions for Exercise 1 and the example addresses aloud.
- Point out that in English, information in an address is ordered from the most specific to the most general.
- Write your own home or school address on the board as an additional example.
- Have students write their own addresses individually. Walk around the classroom, helping students as necessary.
- Call on volunteers to write their addresses on the board.

2
- Read the instructions for Exercise 2 aloud.
- Have students sign their names. They may want to practice several times on a separate sheet of paper.

- Have volunteers sign their names on the board, or pass around a sheet of paper for each student to sign. When all students have signed, post it on the classroom wall.

3
- Read the instructions for Exercise 3 and the example e-mail signature aloud.
- Elicit from students the kind of information that is in the example e-mail signature.
- Have students write their e-mail signatures and compare with a partner or small group.

4
- Read the instructions for Exercise 4 aloud.
- Have students add their address and a signature to their letter from Lesson 6. You can also have students send their letter to you by e-mail.

Unit 2 special places

Overview

In this unit, students write a paragraph about a special place and event from their childhood. They learn to set the scene and write an ending for a personal story.

In the prewriting lessons, students brainstorm and organize details about the place and event. They combine and organize their ideas to write their story in Lesson 6. Lesson 7 gives them additional practice using prepositional phrases to add details to their stories. The *Option: Just for fun* lesson allows visually-oriented students to combine their artistic skills with their writing as they make a tourist guidebook.

	Lesson	Focus	Estimated Time
1	Near my home	Brainstorming	10–20 minutes
2	A special place	Analyzing sentences	10–20 minutes
3	Setting the scene	Learning about organization	15–25 minutes
4	What happened?	Prewriting	25–35 minutes
5	Ending a personal story	Learning about organization	25–35 minutes
6	My special place	Writing	35–45 minutes
7	Prepositional phrases	Editing	20–30 minutes
8	What do you think?	Giving feedback	20–30 minutes
	Tourist guidebook	Option: Just for fun	30–40 minutes

Key points

➤ Make sure students choose to write about a single event that happened at one place and time, such as an accident, party, ceremony, etc. A childhood memory works well.

➤ Students could draw pictures of the scene of their event to help them think of vocabulary and descriptions.

➤ Although the lessons guide the students to think about places and events that happened close to their home, students could also write about events that happened in more distant places.

➤ If you choose to do the *Option: Just for fun* lesson, bring in some English language tourist brochures for students to look at.

➤ Useful language for this unit includes past tenses; the prepositions of place *in, on,* and *at*; and time expressions.

➤ Sections can be skipped. A minimal set of lessons might include 4, 5, and 6.

Lesson 1   Near my home

page 15

Brainstorming

▪ Tell students that they will brainstorm places near their homes where something special or interesting happened to them.

1

▪ Read the instructions for Exercise 1 aloud. Read the words in the box aloud and have the class repeat. Explain vocabulary as necessary.

▪ Have students complete the exercise individually and then compare answers with a partner.

▪ Call on students to give the answers.

> **Answers**
> **1. a.** my best friend's house
>   **b.** the playground
>   **c.** the school
>   **d.** the candy store
>   **e.** the river
>   **f.** the park

2

▪ Call on a student to remind the class what brainstorming is (a method of finding ideas). Explain that writing lists is another method of brainstorming.

▪ Write the following headings on the board: *Special places* and *What happened.*

▪ Read the instructions for Exercise 2 aloud.

▪ Elicit some examples from students and write them on the board. (Possible examples: *playground – broke my arm; park near my house – learned to ride a bicycle.*)

▪ Have students brainstorm to complete the lists individually. Set a time limit of five minutes.

▪ Walk around the classroom, encouraging and helping students as necessary.

3

▪ Read the instructions for Exercise 3 aloud.

▪ Have students compare lists with a partner and add more ideas to their own lists.

▪ Call on some students to read their list of ideas aloud to the class or write them on the board.

Lesson 2   A special place

page 16

Analyzing sentences

▪ Tell students they will look at some typical sentences from a personal story.

1

▪ Read the instructions for Exercise 1 aloud.

▪ Call on students to tell you what they see in the picture. Provide vocabulary as necessary.

▪ Read the instructions for Exercises a–c aloud. Remind students that the topic is the most general subject of the paragraph. If necessary, have students underline the words they will be replacing from sentences 1 and 6.

▪ Have students complete a–c individually.

2

▪ Have students compare answers with a partner.

▪ Call on a student to read the answer to 1a. Call on students to write the answers for 1b–c on the board.

> **Answers**
> **1. a.** falling in a river
>   **b.** There was a park next to my school.
>   **c.** When I arrived at school, my teacher was happy.

Lesson 3 — Setting the scene

page 17

Learning about organization

- Tell students they will learn how to describe the scene of a personal story.
- Read the top of page 17 aloud.

1

- Read the instructions for Exercise 1 aloud.
- Focus students' attention on the picture. Ask them to tell you what they see.
- Read the Word File aloud. Explain vocabulary as necessary.
- Have students complete the exercise individually and then compare answers in small groups.
- Go over answers as a whole class. Write the answers on the board.

Answers
1. a. next to
  b. between
  c. behind
  d. in front of

2

- Read the instructions for Exercise 2 aloud.
- Read the Word File aloud. Explain vocabulary as necessary.
- Have students complete the exercise individually.
- Call on individual students to write the sentences on the board.
- Go over answers as a whole class.

Answers
2. a. When I was
  b. One day
  c. while
  d. After school

Optional activity

Partner writing
Have students work with a partner to write a short story using the expressions in the Word File in Exercise 2. They can work together on each sentence or take turns writing sentences. Encourage them to be creative!

Lesson 4 — What happened?

page 18

Prewriting

- Tell students they will choose an event and place to write about and brainstorm ideas.

1

- Read the instructions for Exercise 1 aloud.
- Give students a few minutes to look back at their lists from Lesson 1 and choose a place and event to write about.
- Walk around the classroom, helping students as necessary.

2

- Read the instructions for Exercise 2 aloud.
- Read Louis's notes aloud. Explain vocabulary as necessary.

- Point out that the last note (*I . . .*) isn't finished. Ask the class to brainstorm ways to finish the sentence, and elicit answers from the class. (Possible answer: I climbed up in the tree to get my glove and cap – and I got stuck!)
- Have students complete the chart for themselves individually. Walk around the classroom, helping students as necessary.

3

- Write the following on the board (as it appears in the text):

  The special place

  When did something important or interesting happen?

  What happened?

- Read the instructions for Exercise 3 and the questions aloud.
- Have students work in groups of three to ask and answer questions about their special place and event.
- After about 15 minutes, or after everyone has had a chance to speak, call on groups to give examples of what students said.

- Ask the class questions such as, *What was the funniest / most unusual story you heard?* Write the examples on the board, filling in the chart. Alternatively, call students in turn to the board to fill out the chart.

Lesson 5	**Ending a personal story**

page 19

Learning about organization

- Tell students they will learn how to write an ending for their stories.
- Read the top of page 19 aloud. Explain vocabulary as necessary.

1

- Read the instructions for Exercise 1 aloud.
- Call on a student to read the information in the box. Explain vocabulary as necessary.
- Have students complete Exercise 1 with a partner.
- Go over answers as a whole class.

> *Answers*
> **1. a.** everyone cheered; proud
>
> **b.** my best friend bought me a new one; happy
>
> **c.** my father was angry; embarrassed

2

- Read the instructions for Exercise 2 aloud.
- Have students complete the exercise individually. Set a time limit of ten minutes.
- If students are having difficulty, elicit examples from one or two students and write them on the board.
- Walk around the classroom, helping students as necessary.
- Call on students to write their story endings on the board or read them aloud. Make corrections as necessary.

> *Answers*
> **2.** Answers will vary. One possible answer: After I fell into the river, my friends ran over to me. I was cold, wet, and embarrassed!

Optional activity

Vocabulary building
Write some more adjectives of feeling on the board, such as disappointed, unhappy, satisfied, delighted, overjoyed. *Have students work with a partner to use their dictionaries to look up the meanings. Then have them come up with concluding sentences, as in Exercise 1 on page 19, that show the meanings of these words.*

- Tell students they will use the information they brainstormed in Lessons 1–5 to write their stories.

1

- Read the instructions for Exercise 1 aloud.
- Have students read the paragraph individually. Remind them that they have read notes for this paragraph in previous lessons.
- Call on students to read the paragraph aloud, sentence by sentence. Explain vocabulary as necessary.
- Have students complete Exercise 1 individually and then compare answers with a partner.
- Go over answers as a whole class.

Answers

1. a. Next to my school there was an old tree.

  b. One day when I was a junior high school student

  c. and There was a bird in the tree, *and* I threw my cap at it.

    but The bird flew away, *but* my cap got stuck in the tree.

    but I threw my baseball glove at the cap, *but* my glove got stuck.

    and Finally, I threw my ball at the bat, *and* even the ball got stuck.

    and I was very embarrassed, *and* my face turned red.

  d. After I told my coach about the tree, he laughed and said, "That tree plays baseball better than you do."

  e. I was very embarrassed, and my face turned red.

Note: This book so far has focused on using *and* and *but* to join sentences. Higher-level students may also mention *when* (*one day* when *I was a junior high school student, I was sitting under the tree* . . . ; *when I threw my bat at the glove, it got stuck, too*) and *after* (*after I told my coach about the tree, he laughed* . . .).

2

- Read the instructions for Exercises 2 and a–b aloud.
- Set a time limit of five to ten minutes for students to draw the picture or map.
- Have students go on to Exercise 2b when they have finished drawing.
- Walk around the classroom, helping students as necessary.

3

- Read the instructions for Exercise 3 aloud.
- Have students write their paragraph on lined paper or type it. Have them skip lines. Tell them you'll collect the paragraphs after they're revised in Lessons 7 and 8.

In your journal . . .

- *If time permits, read the journal entry instructions aloud. Tell students to use language from the first Word File in Lesson 3, if they can.*
- *Students can write in class or at home.*

■ Tell students they will learn to use prepositional phrases to add more details to a story.

■ Have a student read the sentence on the top of page 22.

1

■ Read the instructions for Exercise 1 aloud.

■ Have a student read the prepositional phrases aloud. Explain vocabulary as necessary. If students have questions about the prepositions, draw pictures on the board to explain them.

■ Have students work individually to complete the exercise and then compare answers with a partner.

■ Check answers by calling on students to read the sentences aloud.

Answers

1. When I was ten years old, my family and I spent a year **in Australia**. We lived **in a small town** called Steele. Something interesting happened there that makes me laugh even today. My brother and I went to a small school **at the end of our street**. One day **at school** when we were sitting **on a bench** in the schoolyard, my brother started laughing, and said, "Look over

---

there! There's a kangaroo." A kangaroo was lying in front of the bus stop **on the sidewalk**. It was trying to keep cool in the shade. Just then a man **on a bicycle** rode by. The man was riding in the street, but he was so surprised that he fell off of the bicycle. He fell on top of the kangaroo. The kangaroo jumped up and hopped away toward the park. Then the kangaroo lay down under some trees **in the park** and fell asleep.

2

■ Read the instructions for Exercise 2 aloud.

■ Have students work in class or at home to complete Exercise 2.

■ Call on students who made changes to their paragraphs to write their original sentences and their revisions on the board.

Optional activity

Group story writing
Have students work in groups. Have them make a list of five to seven prepositional phrases. Each group passes their phrases to the next group, which collectively writes a short story incorporating as many of the phrases as possible. Groups read their stories aloud to the class. Encourage students to be creative!

■ Tell students that they are going to read each other's paragraphs and that they will need a sheet of paper for Exercise 2.

1

■ Read the instructions for Exercises 1 and a–b aloud.

■ Have students exchange their paragraphs with a partner and complete Exercises a–b individually. Walk around the classroom, helping students as necessary.

■ When they finish, tell them to exchange books and review their partner's answers. They can then go on to Exercise 2.

2

■ Read the instructions for Exercise 2 aloud. Then call on a student to read the example letter.

■ Have students write their letters to their partner individually.

■ Walk around the classroom, helping students as necessary.

3

- Read the instructions for Exercise 3 aloud.
- Have students give their letters to their partner.
- Give students time to tell their partner the answer to any questions in the letter.

Option	Tourist guidebook

page 24 **Just for fun**

- Ask students, *How many of you like to travel? How many of you have used a guidebook?*
- Tell students that they are going to write a guidebook for their town or the town they're currently living in.

1

- Read the instructions for Exercise 1 aloud, including the examples in the chart.
- Have students brainstorm a list of activities in groups. All students should think of ideas, and one secretary in each group can write them down.
- Walk around the classroom, helping students as necessary.
- Write three columns titled *Children, Teenagers,* and *Adults* on the board. Write or have a student write some of the answers groups suggest.

Answers

1. Answers will vary. Possible answers:

Children: a. Play on the playground equipment in the park. b. Climb on the rocks around the lake. c. Visit the children's museum downtown.

Teenagers: a. Go to the video arcade. b. Go to the movie theater. c. Play mini-golf.

Adults: a. Have coffee with your friends. b. Eat delicious snacks. c. Look at the local artwork on the coffee shop walls.

- Have students revise their paragraphs based on the comments they receive and other ideas they have. They can complete their revisions either in class or at home.
- Have students turn in their revised paragraphs to you.

2

- Read the instructions for Exercise 2 and the example sentences aloud.
- Have students take turns writing sentences for the guidebook. Alternatively, have all students think of sentences while one secretary writes them down.

3

- Read the instructions for Exercise 3 aloud. Use the pictures to explain the instructions.
- Have a student demonstrate how to fold the paper while you read the instructions.
- Have students complete their guidebooks in class or at home. Encourage them to be creative.

4

- Have each group give a presentation about their guidebooks. You may want to hang up the guidebooks to display in the classroom, or share them with another class.

Unit 3 An ideal partner

Overview

In this unit, students write a paragraph about the kind of person they would like as a partner. They learn how to put information in order and give reasons.

In the prewriting lessons, students describe preferences, values, and personality characteristics. They learn to support their opinions by giving reasons, and to organize information in a paragraph with transition words such as *first*, *second,* and *third*. In Lesson 6, students combine their work from the prewriting lessons into a paragraph. The postwriting editing lesson on parallel structure helps students combine sentences to make their writing more interesting. The *Option: Just for fun* lesson has students review writing about people with an enjoyable game.

	Lesson	Focus	Estimated Time
1	Characteristics of a partner	Brainstorming	15–25 minutes
2	An ideal partner	Analyzing sentences	10–20 minutes
3	Ideal partner interview	Prewriting	15–25 minutes
4	Putting information in order	Learning about organization	15–25 minutes
5	Giving reasons I	Learning about organization	25–35 minutes
6	My ideal partner	Writing	30–40 minutes
7	Parallel structure	Editing	20–30 minutes
8	What do you think?	Giving feedback	20–30 minutes
	Dating game	Option: Just for fun	30–40 minutes

Key points

➤ This unit is rich in vocabulary to describe personalities and characteristics. Encourage students to learn additional words that are meaningful to them.

➤ If describing a romantic partner is inappropriate for some or all of your class, make the partner a business partner, roommate, or friend instead.

➤ Useful language for this unit includes *I want a partner who (is tall), I want a partner who (is tall) because (I am tall),* and *want/would like.*

➤ Sections can be skipped. A minimal set of lessons might include 3, 4, 5, and 6.

page 25

Lesson 1 — Characteristics of a partner

- Before doing Exercise 1, define "ideal partner." Tell the class, *An ideal partner is someone who is – or would be – perfect for you. It is someone you would like to be romantically involved with, like a boyfriend or girlfriend, or a husband or wife.*

1

- Read the instructions for Exercise 1 aloud. Explain that "characteristics" refer to what a person is like. Write these examples on the board: *is intelligent, has a good sense of humor, is hardworking.*
- Call on a student to read the six characteristics aloud. Explain vocabulary as necessary.
- Have students complete the exercise individually.
- Have students compare answers in small groups or with a partner.

- Go over answers as a whole class by asking, *Is (being rich) an important characteristic in an ideal partner?* and have students raise their hands.

2

- Read the instructions for Exercise 2 aloud.
- Have students brainstorm individually. Set a time limit of three to five minutes.
- Walk around the classroom, helping students as necessary. You may need to provide additional vocabulary.

3

- Read the instructions for Exercise 3 aloud.
- Have students compare lists with a partner and add more ideas to their own lists.
- Call on some students to read their list of ideas aloud to the class or write them on the board.

Lesson 2 — An ideal partner

page 26

1

- Read the instructions for Exercise 1 aloud.
- Have students read the paragraph individually.
- Call on students to read the paragraph aloud, sentence by sentence. Provide vocabulary as necessary.
- Read the instructions for a–d aloud.
- Have students complete a–d individually or with a partner.
- If students are having difficulty, you may want to stop after 1b and go over the answers.
- Ask students to raise their hands or nod at you to let you know when they have finished.

2

- Have students compare answers with a partner.
- Write or have individual students write answers on the board. Point out the commas after *First* and *Third*.

Answers

1. a. First, Second, Third

    b. because I am very outgoing

    c. First, I want a partner who likes animals.

    d. Third, I would like someone who can play tennis.

Optional activity

Substitution game

Write the paragraph on the board with the following words underlined:

What kind of partner do I want? First, I want a partner who can <u>speak English</u>. Second, I want a partner who likes <u>to go to parties</u> because I <u>am very outgoing</u>. Third, I would like someone who likes <u>to travel</u>.

Students take turns reading the sentences aloud, substituting different words for the underlined ones. If necessary, prepare by brainstorming a list of common likes with the whole class.

page 27

Prewriting

- Tell students they will interview a classmate to find out about his or her ideal partner.

1

- Read the instructions for Exercise 1 aloud.
- Have a student read the example sentences aloud.
- Read the characteristics in a–j aloud and have the class repeat. Check understanding of the vocabulary by eliciting definitions or examples from students. Explain vocabulary as necessary.
- Model the interview by calling on two students. Say, *Maria, ask Nina the first question.* Maria asks, *Nina, do you want a partner who is playful or who is serious?* Nina responds, *I want a partner who is serious*, and marks her own answer on the chart.
- Have students complete the interview with a classmate.
- Walk around the classroom, helping students as necessary.

2

- Read the instructions for Exercise 2 aloud.
- Have students stand up and talk to several other classmates.
- After five to ten minutes, have students return to their seats and write their answer.

- Ask students about the responses they got from their classmates. You might ask, *Which response was most interesting to you?* or *Which response surprised you the most?*
- Call on volunteers to write their sentences on the board. While they are writing, walk around the room and check the sentences that the others wrote.

> **Answers**
> **2.** Answers will vary. One possible answer: I want a partner who is talkative, likes sports, and cares about fashion.

Optional activity

Class survey: The top five characteristics we want!
Write Our ideal partner on the board. Ask students to brainstorm the most important characteristics of an ideal partner and write them on the board. Have students vote for their favorites. Mark their answers and circle the five most popular characteristics. Then, as a class, write sentences about the class ideal partner (e.g., We would like someone who has a great job, is athletic, likes dancing, etc.). You may want to make separate lists for men and women.

---

page 28

Learning about organization

- Have a student read the top of page 28 aloud.

1

- Read the instructions for Exercise 1 aloud.
- Call on a student to read the paragraph aloud. Explain vocabulary as necessary.
- Have students complete the exercise individually.
- Call on students to read their answers. Write or have a student write the sentences on the board. If possible, use a colored marker or piece of chalk to insert *First*, *Second*, and *Third*.

> **Answers**
> **1.**   What kind of partner do I want? **First**, I want a partner who has a car. **Second**, I would like a partner who doesn't have pets. I don't like pets. **Third**, I would like a partner who comes from a different country. I would like to live abroad some day.

2

- Read the instructions for Exercise 2 aloud.
- Point out that in this situation, *want* and *would like* have the same meaning. Students should use both expressions to add variety to their writing.

- Have students complete Exercise 2 individually.
- Call on students to share their examples with the class by reading them aloud or writing them on the board.

> **Answers**
>
> **2.** Answers will vary. Possible answers:
>
> | is ambitious | I want a partner who is ambitious. |
> | can dance | I would like a partner who can dance. |
> | likes children | I would like a partner who likes children. |

3

- Read the instructions for Exercise 3 aloud.
- Tell students to write the most important characteristic first, the next most important characteristic second, etc.
- Have students complete the exercise individually. Walk around the classroom, helping students as necessary.

> **Answers**
>
> **3.** Answers will vary. Possible answer:
> First, I want a partner who is ambitious. Second, I would like a partner who can dance. Third, I would like a partner who likes children.

| Lesson 5 | **Giving reasons 1** |

Learning about organization

- Tell students that giving support – more information, explanations, and details – makes their writing stronger.
- Have a student read the top of page 29 aloud.
- Have another student read the example. Explain that what comes after *because* supports what came before it by giving a reason. This helps readers understand your ideas more easily.

1

- Read the instructions for Exercise 1 aloud.
- Have students individually complete a–d. For lower-level classes, do 1a together as a class, and write the answer on the board.
- Go over answers as a whole class. Write or have individual students write the sentences on the board. Ask, *Does anyone have similar interests or desires for his or her partner?*

> **Answers**
>
> **a.** I want a partner who cares about fashion because I like to wear nice clothes.
>
> **b.** I would like a partner who likes sports because I play tennis a lot.

> **c.** I would like a partner who doesn't tell lies because I had a partner once who lied to me and hurt me.
>
> **d.** I want a partner who likes children because I want to have a big family.

2

- Read the instructions for Exercise 2 and the example sentence aloud.
- Have students work on a–c individually.
- Walk around the classroom, helping students as necessary.
- Have volunteers write their sentences on the board or read them aloud.

> **Optional activity**
>
> *Group review*
> *Have students work in small groups. Have each student share the sentences they wrote in Exercise 2. As a group, they vote on their favorite sentence. (It could be the most interesting because it's funny, unusual, surprising, etc.) Have a representative from each group write the sentence on the board and explain to the class why they thought it was interesting.*

My ideal partner

pages 30–31   **Writing**

1

- Read the instructions for Exercise 1 aloud.
- Have students read the paragraph individually.
- Call on students to read the paragraph aloud. Explain vocabulary as necessary.
- Have students complete a–c individually or with a partner.
- Go over answers as a whole class.

> **Answers**
> **a.** First, Second, Third.
> **b.** who likes sports, who likes being with groups of people, who comes from a different country
> **c.** want, would like

2

- Read the instructions for Exercise 2 aloud, including *Write these things* and the cues that follow.

- Have students complete the exercise individually. Remind them that they have discussed and written the information in previous lessons. However, they may write new information if they wish.
- Walk around the classroom, helping students as necessary.

3

- Have students write their paragraph on lined paper or type it. Have them skip lines. Tell them you'll collect the paragraphs after they're revised in Lessons 7 and 8.

> **In your journal . . .**
>
> - *If time permits, read the journal entry instructions aloud. Tell students they can write about different ideas for the ideal day as well. Have them use the structures* I want to *and* I would like to.
> - *Students can write in class or at home.*

Parallel structure

page 32   **Editing**

- Tell students that we often combine sentences when possible to make writing more interesting.
- Have students take turns reading the information and examples on top of page 32. Point out how the sentences that are combined are ones with similar structures.

1

- Read the instructions for Exercise 1 aloud.
- Call on a student to read the paragraph aloud. Explain vocabulary as necessary.
- Have students complete the exercise individually. Remind them to look for sentences next to each other that have the same verbs.
- Go over answers as a whole class.

> **Answers**
> **1.** I like swimming. I also like sailing.
>
> I prefer staying at home. I prefer being alone with my partner.
>
> I like watching TV with my partner. I also like listening to music with my partner.
>
> Third, I hope my partner is quiet. I also hope my partner is a good listener.

2

- Read the instructions for Exercise 2 and the example sentence aloud.
- Have students work individually or with a partner to complete the exercise. If students work with a partner, have them decide on an answer together, and then each write the answer in their books.
- Go over answers by having students come to the board and write the answers.

3

- Read the instructions for Exercise 3 aloud.

- Have students who want to combine sentences revise their paragraphs from Lesson 6 in class or at home.

- Have students share their revisions in groups or have volunteers write their old and new sentences on the board.

Lesson 8	**What do you think?**

page 33   **Giving feedback**

- Tell students that they are going to read each other's paragraphs and that they will need a sheet of paper for Exercise 2.

1

- Read the instructions for Exercises 1 and a–c aloud.

- Have students exchange their paragraphs with a classmate and complete Exercises a–c individually. Walk around the classroom, helping students as necessary.

- When they finish, ask the class, *In c, how many people checked (artist)?* See which was the most popular partner chosen. Ask how many people wrote their own ideas, and what they were.

- Tell students to exchange books and review their classmate's answers.

2

- Read the instructions for Exercise 2 aloud. Then call on a student to read the example letter.

- Have students write their letters to their partner individually.

- Walk around the classroom, helping students as necessary.

3

- Read the instructions for Exercise 3 aloud.

- Have students give their letters to their partner.

- Have students revise their paragraphs based on the comments they receive and other ideas they have. They can complete their revisions either in class or at home.

- Have students turn in their revised paragraphs to you.

Option	**Dating game**

page 34   **Just for fun**

- If you have a large class, divide them into smaller groups of 8–10 students to play the game.

- A table or group of flat desks pushed together is useful.

- Tell students that they will need a sheet of paper for Exercise 1.

- Ask, *Do you know what a dating game is?* Have students who have seen dating games on TV describe them to the class.

1

- Read the instructions for Exercises 1 and a–d aloud.

- Point out the model character profile sheet.

- Have students work alone or with a partner to complete Exercises a–d.

- Make sure each group is creating an equal number of male and female characters. If necessary, assign a gender to each student or pair's character.

- Walk around the classroom, encouraging and helping students as necessary.

2

- Read the instructions for Exercise 2a aloud and have students carry them out before you continue.

- Read the instructions for Exercises b–c aloud, and answer any questions before continuing. To check comprehension, ask a student to explain the instructions again.

- Give students about ten minutes to read the character profiles and write down who they think would best match their character. If students created a character with a partner, the pair makes this decision together.

3

- Have each student (or one student from each pair) point to the partner his or her character chose.

- Ask the groups if there were any matches.

- Have students role-play their characters. Have the matched couples explain why they chose each other, and ask a few characters who couldn't get partners for comments about their choices.

Overview

In this unit, students write a paragraph to describe one of their favorite photos. In addition, they learn how to begin and end their paragraph.

In the prewriting lessons, students learn to begin a paragraph with general information, add supporting sentences that give details about their photos, and write a concluding sentence that summarizes the paragraph. In the postwriting lesson, students decide whether information in their paragraph should be written in the present or the past tense. The *Option: Just for fun* lesson lets students extend and develop the skills they practiced in the unit by writing about several important events in their life.

	Lesson	Focus	Estimated Time
I	Photos	Brainstorming	10–20 minutes
2	A favorite photo	Analyzing sentences	10–20 minutes
3	General information	Learning about organization	15–25 minutes
4	Photo facts	Prewriting	20–30 minutes
5	Writing a concluding sentence	Learning about organization	15–25 minutes
6	My favorite photo	Writing	30–40 minutes
7	Present or past?	Editing	15–25 minutes
8	What do you think?	Giving feedback	20–30 minutes
	Picture autobiography	Option: Just for fun	40–50 minutes

Key points

➤ Remember to tell students beforehand to bring two or three of their favorite photos to class to use in Lesson 3 and afterwards. Have students who forget to bring photos or don't have any draw pictures.

➤ Encourage students to choose photos where something is happening, rather than photos of people just standing. They should know the people in the photo well enough to write about them.

➤ Useful language for this unit includes the simple present and simple past tenses.

➤ Sections can be skipped. A minimal set of lessons might include 3, 4, 5, and 6.

24

■ Ask, *What does "snapshot" mean? What other words mean the same thing?* (Answers: photograph, photo, shot, picture.)

1

■ Read the instructions for Exercise 1 aloud.

■ Call on students to read the captions from the photo album. Explain vocabulary as necessary by using the pictures.

■ Have students complete Exercise 1 individually.

■ Go over responses as a whole class by reading each caption and having students raise their hand if they checked it.

2

■ Read the instructions for Exercise 2 aloud. Point out that students can write notes instead of complete sentences.

■ Have students complete the exercise individually. Set a time limit of three to five minutes.

page 35   **Brainstorming**

3

■ Read the instructions for Exercise 3 aloud.

■ Have students compare lists with a partner and add more ideas to their own lists.

■ Call on some students to read their list of ideas aloud to the class or write them on the board.

Optional activity

Class survey of popular photos
Have students work in groups. Have one person be the group's secretary. Students make a list of types of photos that they all have (e.g., a high school graduation, birthday party, etc.) and then guess what the five most popular class photos are. Check answers by calling on students from each group to write their lists and guesses on the board. See which group had the most accurate list of the class's five most popular photos.

1

■ Read the instructions for Exercise 1 aloud.

■ Have students read the paragraph individually.

■ Call on students to read the paragraph aloud, sentence by sentence. Explain vocabulary as necessary.

■ Read the instructions for Exercises a–d aloud.

■ Have students complete a–d individually.

■ Walk around the classroom, helping students as necessary.

■ If your students are having a difficult time, you may want to stop after 1b and review.

■ Ask students to raise their hands or nod at you when they have finished.

2

■ Have students compare answers with a partner.

■ Call on students to write the answers on the board.

page 36   **Analyzing sentences**

Answers
1. a. my friends and me; on my 21st birthday

   b. I like the photo because it reminds me of how much I love my friends.

   c. My favorite photo is of my family and me on New Year's Day.

   d. I like the photo because it reminds me of my family.

Optional activity

Photo album
Have students bring in a photo album to show classmates. Divide the class into small groups. Students take turns showing a few photos from their albums. Tell students to use the language in Lesson 2 to discuss their photos. Group members can ask questions about the photos. After about ten minutes, call on students to tell the class what they learned about their classmates.

■ Read the top of page 37 aloud.

■ Call on a student to read the example sentences aloud.

1

■ Read the instructions for Exercise 1 aloud.

■ Ask the class, *What do you see in photo (a, b, c)?* Provide vocabulary as necessary.

■ Read the answer choices for Exercises a–c aloud.

■ Have students complete a–c individually.

■ Go over answers as a whole class.

■ Make sure you point out why the answer is correct. Students need to identify the sentence that tells who is in the photo and when it was taken.

Answers

1. a. My favorite photo was taken the day my brother and I went to Water World.

b. My favorite photo is of my parents on their wedding day.

c. My favorite photo was taken when my soccer team won the championship.

2

■ Read the instructions for Exercise 2 aloud.

■ Have students complete the exercise individually.

■ Walk around the classroom, encouraging and helping students as necessary. You may want to take additional class time to correct errors with individual sentences, or you can have students compare their answers with a partner.

■ Tell students to bring their favorite photo to class to write about in the next lesson, if possible.

Optional activity

Match the photo
Bring photos from magazines or the Internet of famous people or people doing interesting things. Have students work with a partner. Give each pair one or two photos. Have each pair write a general sentence that describes the photo on a slip of paper. They should use their imagination. Post the photos around the room. Collect the sentences, mix them up, and give a new one to each pair. Have pairs stand up and move around the room to find the photo that matches their sentence. The first pair to find the match wins.

■ If students did not bring photos to class, have them draw pictures or use their imagination.

1

■ Read the instructions for Exercise 1 aloud.

■ Call on individual students to read the headings in the boxes and the example phrases and sentences.

■ Ask, *Why are the details important?* (Possible answers: Because they make the descriptions more interesting; Because they add information.)

■ Have students complete their charts individually. Walk around the classroom, helping students as necessary.

■ If students are having difficulty, draw the chart on the board, call a student to the board, and complete the chart together.

2

■ Have students compare their charts with a partner.

■ Give students time to add information to their charts.

Optional activity

Boring or exciting?
Have students work with a partner. Give each pair a photo. (You can use students' photos or the pictures from the Optional activity in Lesson 3.) Tell pairs to write two descriptions for each photo: one that's boring and one that's exciting. Then pairs read their descriptions to the class. The class says which description is boring and which description is exciting. Encourage students to read with expression.

page 39

■ Read the top of page 39 aloud.

■ Call on a student to read the examples.

1

■ Read the instructions for Exercise 1 aloud.

■ Call on students to read the choices for a–d aloud. Explain vocabulary as necessary.

■ Have students work with a partner to complete a–d.

■ Go over answers as a whole class. Discuss why the other sentences are not good concluding sentences.

Answers

1. a. This photo helps me remember our trip to the Grand Canyon.

   b. This photo reminds me of the first time I saw snow.

   c. When I look at this photo, I remember our wonderful play.

   d. I like this photo because it helps me remember the years I lived in Japan.

2

■ Read the instruction for Exercise 2 aloud.

■ Have students complete the exercise individually. Walk around the classroom, helping students as necessary.

■ Have students compare sentences with a partner.

■ Call on some students to write their sentences on the board.

Optional activity

Concluding sentences about paintings

Bring copies of several paintings from magazines or the Internet. If your students are imaginative, use abstract as well as representational paintings. Have students work with a partner. Give each pair a painting (you can give a copy of the same painting to more than one pair). Have students write a concluding sentence like the ones in Lesson 5 about the painting. Write this useful language on the board:

   What does this painting remind you of?

   I like this painting because it reminds me of . . .

   This painting helps me to remember . . .

   When I look at this painting, I remember . . .

Encourage students to be creative! Have pairs share their sentences with other pairs.

Lesson 6   **My favorite photo**

Writing

page 40

1

■ Read the instructions for Exercise 1 aloud.

■ Ask, *What do you see in the photo?* Provide vocabulary as necessary.

■ Have students read the paragraph individually.

■ Call on students to read the paragraph aloud. Explain vocabulary as necessary.

■ Read the instructions for Exercises a–c aloud.

■ Have students complete a–c individually or with a partner.

■ Go over answers as a whole class.

Answers

1. a. My favorite photo is of my grandparents on the day they met. It was taken in 1950 at the beach in Brooklyn, New York.

   b. This photo is special to me because it helps me to remember my grandparents. It also reminds me that sometimes when something unlucky happens, good people meet each other.

   c. They were both smiling because my grandfather rescued my grandmother from the ocean. She was standing in the water and slipped. She couldn't swim, so he picked her up and brought her to shore. I think that was the day they fell in love.

In your journal . . .

- *If time permits, read the journal entry instructions aloud. If students don't have a camera, they can write about why not or write about what kind of photos or artwork they like to look at.*

- *Students can write in class or at home.*

2

- Read the instructions for Exercise 2 aloud, including *Remember to write* and the cues that follow.

- Have students write their paragraph on lined paper or type it. Have them skip lines. Tell them you'll collect the paragraphs after they're revised in Lessons 7 and 8.

Lesson 7   Present or past?

Editing

page 41

- Read the information and examples on top of page 41 aloud.

- For higher-level classes, point out examples of the past progressive from the model in Lesson 6 (*They were both smiling . . .* ; *She was standing in the water. . . .*).

1

- Ask, *What do you see in the photo?* Provide vocabulary as necessary.

- Read the instructions for Exercise 1 aloud.

- Read the paragraph aloud, with the verbs in the base form. Explain vocabulary as necessary.

- Have students complete the exercise individually or with a partner.

- Check answers by calling on students to read the sentences aloud.

Answers
1.   My favorite photo **is** of me and my family in Egypt. We **took** a trip to the Temple of Karnak in Luxor a few years ago. One day, my brother and I **walked** around a temple. We **pretended** we were in a James Bond movie and **hid** from the guards. It **was** so fun. I **asked** one of the guards to take our picture. This photo **reminds** me of our spy game in that exotic place. Whenever I see that photo, I **smile**.

2

- Read the instructions for Exercise 2 aloud.

- Have students check their paragraphs from Lesson 6 in class or at home and revise as necessary.

- Have students share their revisions in groups or have volunteers write their old and new sentences on the board.

Lesson 8   What do you think?

Giving feedback

page 42

- Tell students that they are going to read each other's paragraphs and that they will need a sheet of paper for Exercise 2.

1

- Read the instructions for Exercises 1 and a–b aloud.

- Have students exchange their paragraphs with a partner and complete Exercises a–b individually. Walk around the classroom, helping students as necessary.

- Tell students to exchange books and review their partner's answers.

2

- Read the instructions for Exercise 2 aloud. Then call on a student to read the example letter.
- Have students write their letters to their partner individually.
- Walk around the classroom, helping students as necessary.

3

- Read the instructions for Exercise 3 aloud.
- Have students give their letters to their partner. Give them time to tell their partner the answer to the question in the letter.

- Have students revise their paragraphs based on the comments they receive and other ideas they have. They can complete their revisions either in class or at home.
- Have students turn in their revised paragraphs to you.

Optional activity

Class photo gallery
Set up a display area on a wall either in the classroom or in the hall. Have students bring in another favorite photo to write about. Have them write sentences or paragraphs about the photos on index cards. Put interested students in charge of creating the display.

Option | **Picture autobiography**

page 43 **Just for fun**

- Ask students if they know what *autobiography* means. (Answer: A story of someone's life, written by that person.) Tell students they will use pictures to create an autobiography.
- If students don't have childhood photos, they can draw pictures.
- Students will need large pieces of paper or poster board and colored pencils or markers.

I

- Read the instructions for Exercise 1 aloud.
- Call on different students to read the information in the time line aloud. Explain vocabulary as necessary.

2

- Read the instructions for Exercise 2 aloud.
- Have students complete the chart individually.

3

- Read instructions for Exercise 3 aloud.
- Distribute poster paper to the class.
- Have students complete the exercise individually.

4

- Read the instructions for Exercise 4 aloud.
- Call on a student to read the example.
- Have students write their descriptions individually.
- Walk around the classroom, helping students as necessary.

5

- Have students take turns explaining their time lines to the class.
- Ask students what interesting things they learned about each other.

Optional activity

Writing about classmates
Have students write in their journal about their classmates' time lines. They can answer the following questions: What was the most surprising thing you learned about your classmates? Which one was most similar to yours? Explain!

29

Unit 5 My seal

Overview

In this unit, students design a personal seal and write a paragraph explaining the position and meaning of the symbols they chose. They also learn how to write topic sentences.

In the prewriting lessons, students brainstorm symbols that represent their interests and personalities. They use prepositions of place to describe the organization of their seals. The central writing assignment of the unit in Lesson 6 combines their drawn seal with a written description. The postwriting lesson shows students how to move clauses with *because* to the beginning of a sentence to add variety to their writing. The *Option: Just for fun* lesson gives students further practice with the same concepts and language as they design a flag with a group.

	Lesson	Focus	Estimated Time
1	Thinking about me	Brainstorming	15–25 minutes
2	Three symbols	Analyzing sentences	10–20 minutes
3	Choosing symbols	Prewriting	15–25 minutes
4	Designing a seal	Prewriting	25–35 minutes
5	Topic sentences	Learning about organization	15–25 minutes
6	My seal	Writing	30–40 minutes
7	Commas with *because*	Editing	20–30 minutes
8	What do you think?	Giving feedback	20–30 minutes
	Group flag	Option: Just for fun	30–40 minutes

Key points

➤ Bring some seals, flags, or logos to the first class. Show how they are made of symbols. You can use seals from companies, political organizations, companies, sports teams, etc. Many of these can be found on the Internet.

➤ Some students might take a long time to design their seal, so you should either leave ample class time or assign the seal design as homework.

➤ If students draw their seals in class, ask them to bring colored pencils or markers.

➤ Useful language for this unit includes prepositions of place and the connector *because*.

➤ Sections can be skipped. A minimal set of lessons might include 3, 4, 5, and 6.

page 44

Brainstorming

1

- Read the instructions for Exercise 1 aloud. Ask students to tell you what they see in the seal. Provide vocabulary as necessary.
- Read the information in the box and sentences in a–d aloud.
- Have students complete the exercise individually and then compare answers with a partner.
- Go over answers as a whole class.

Answers

1. a. strength

   b. study

   c. sports

   d. many cultures together

2

- Read the instructions for Exercise 2 aloud.
- Call on a student to read the different categories and examples in the chart.
- Have students complete Exercise 2 individually. Set a time limit of five minutes.
- Walk around the classroom, helping students as necessary.

3

- Read the instructions for Exercise 3 aloud.
- Have students compare lists with a partner and add more ideas to their own lists.
- Call on some students to read their list of ideas aloud to the class or write them on the board.

page 45

Analyzing sentences

1

- Read the instructions for Exercise 1 aloud.
- Have students read the paragraph individually.
- Call on students to read the paragraph aloud, sentence by sentence. Have the rest of the class point to the symbol on the seal as the appropriate sentence is read. Explain vocabulary as necessary.
- Point out the colon [:] in sentence 1 and the dash [–] in sentence 3. These punctuation marks show that an example or explanation will follow. A guitar and four stars are examples of two symbols, and playing rock music is an explanation of a dream.
- Read the instructions for Exercises a–c aloud.

- Have students complete a–c individually.
- Walk around the classroom, helping students as necessary.
- Ask students to raise their hands or nod to let you know when they have finished.

2

- Have students compare answers with a partner.
- Elicit answers from the class.
- Call on students to write the sentences from 1b–c on the board. Check to see that a colon was used in 1b and a dash in 1c.
- Point out the use of commas in a list of three items, as in 1b (a pen, a rose, and two hearts).

Optional activity

Sports team symbols

Have students work in small groups. Have them brainstorm five different sports teams with symbols or logos they know. Write this pattern on the board as a model: The symbol of the soccer team Real Madrid is a crown. We think the crown represents power. *Groups may need to use dictionaries or ask you for help with vocabulary. Artistic students could draw pictures of the symbols as well. When they are finished, have each group present their ideas to the class. Do the other class members agree with the interpretation? When all the groups are finished, ask students which symbols they like the best.*

Lesson 3	Choosing symbols

Prewriting

page 46

1

- Read the instructions for Exercise 1 aloud.
- Call on students to read the examples in the chart. Explain vocabulary as necessary.
- Have students complete Exercise 1 individually.
- Walk around the classroom, helping students as necessary. Students may need to use their dictionaries or ask your help to find the name of the plant or animal they want.

2

- Read the instructions for Exercise 2 aloud.
- Call on two students to read the model interview.
- Give students some time to plan what they are going to say.

- Have students interview each other, using the model as a guide.
- Call on students to share the information they learned in the interview.

3

- Read the instructions for Exercise 3 aloud. Point out that they are writing down the same information they gave in their interviews.
- Have students complete Exercise 3 individually.
- Walk around the classroom, helping students as necessary.
- Call on some students to write their sentences on the board. Walk around the classroom to check other students' sentences.

Lesson 4	Designing a seal

Prewriting

page 47

- You may want to bring or ask students to bring colored pencils or markers to make their seals.

1

- Read the instructions for Exercises 1 and a–b.
- Have students complete a–b individually.
- Walk around the classroom, encouraging and helping students as necessary.
- If some students are reluctant to draw in their books, have them draw on a separate sheet of paper.
- Have students share their seals in small groups.

2

- Read the instructions for Exercise 2 and the Word File aloud.
- If students are not already familiar with the vocabulary in the Word File, explain it by drawing simple pictures on the board.
- Have students complete a–c individually.
- Go over answers as a whole class.

3

- Read the instructions for Exercise 3 aloud.
- Have students complete the exercise individually.
- Have students compare answers with a partner. Walk around the classroom, helping students as necessary and checking their work.

Lesson 5	**Topic sentences**

page 48 **Learning about organization**

- Read the information about topic sentences at the top of page 48 aloud.
- Call on a student to read the examples aloud.
- Tell students that topic sentences help the writer create a more organized paragraph and also help the reader easily understand the writer's main idea.

1

- Read the instructions for Exercise 1 aloud.
- Have a student read the words from the box aloud. Explain vocabulary as necessary.
- Have students work with a partner to complete the exercise. Encourage students to guess if they are not sure of the answer.
- Go over answers as a whole class.

Answers
1. In England, a red rose represents **the Queen**. In Germany, an apple represents **knowledge**. In Japan, a chrysanthemum represents **the royal family**. In the United States, an "H" represents **a hospital**. In China, the number eight represents **good luck**.

2

- Read the instructions for Exercise 2 aloud.
- Call on students to read the three sentences aloud.

- Ask a volunteer which one would be the best topic sentence.
- Write the answer on the board, and ask why the other answers would not be good topic sentences. (Answer: The other sentences don't introduce the main idea of this paragraph.)

Answer
2. There are many different symbols around the world.

3

- Read the instructions for Exercise 3 aloud.
- Have students complete the exercise individually.
- Go over the answer as a whole class.
- Discuss with the class why the other sentences would not be good topic sentences for that paragraph.

Answer
3. My seal has three symbols: a cactus, stars, and an airplane.

4

- Read the instructions for Exercise 4 aloud.
- Have students work individually to write their sentences.
- Elicit examples from the class and write them on the board.

Optional activity

Other common symbols

Have students work in groups to brainstorm other symbols they know. Together, have them write an exercise that looks like Exercise 1 in Lesson 5. Then have groups exchange exercises with another group and do one another's exercise. When they finish, they should add a topic sentence and then hand it back to the writers to correct.

Lesson 6   My seal

Writing

page 49

1

- Read the instructions for Exercise 1 aloud.
- Ask students to tell you what they see in the seal. Provide vocabulary as necessary.
- Have students read the paragraph individually.
- Call on students to read the paragraph aloud. If necessary, use a world map to show where Costa Rica and Canada are.
- Read the instructions for a–c aloud.
- Have students complete a–c individually or with a partner.
- Go over answers as a whole class.

Answers

1. a. My seal has four symbols: a pine tree, wheels, a sun, and snow.

  b. in the center, below the tree, above the tree on the right, on the left

  c. pine tree: a character that never changes

    wheels: his motorcycle

    sun: Costa Rica

    snow: Canada

2

- Read the instructions for Exercise 2 aloud, including *Remember to write* and the cues that follow.
- Have students write their paragraph on lined paper or type it. Have them skip lines. If they wish, they can draw their seal on a separate sheet and attach it. Tell them you'll collect the paragraphs after they're revised in Lessons 7 and 8.

In your journal . . .

- *If time permits, read the journal entry instructions aloud. Encourage students to use language from the unit if they can. They can also write about what different colors represent in their cultures (e.g., In my country, purple represents royalty.).*
- *Students can write in class or at home.*

Lesson 7   Commas with *because*

Editing

page 50

- Write the word *because* on the board.
- Have students give you some example sentences using *because*. They could use examples from their paragraphs from Lesson 6.
- Read the information and example sentences at the top of page 50 aloud.

- Explain that the position of *because* does not change the meaning of the sentence. Encourage students to use *because* in both positions to add variety to their writing.
- Read the second example sentence again, pausing after the first clause to demonstrate why a comma is used there.

- Read the instructions for Exercise 1 aloud.
- Call on students to read the sentences in a–j aloud. Explain vocabulary as necessary.
- Have students complete b–j individually.
- Walk around the classroom, helping students as necessary.
- Have students compare answers with a partner.
- Go over answers as a whole class.

> **Answers**
> **1. a.** Because I love singing, my seal has musical notes around the edge.
> **b.** The gold coin represents my father because he always gives me money.
> **c.** Because I am small and strong, I chose an ant to represent myself.
> **d.** Because I love plants and trees, the main color of my seal is green.
> **e.** Because my hobby is sailing, I drew ocean waves at the bottom.

> **f.** My best friend drew my seal because I'm very bad at drawing.
> **g.** A rabbit represents my character because a rabbit is quiet and friendly.
> **h.** The bird represents my school baseball team because we are called the Eagles.
> **i.** Because music is the most important thing in my life, there is a piano in the center of my seal.
> **j.** There are many colors in my seal because I like painting.

2
- Read the instructions for Exercise 2 aloud.
- Have students check their paragraphs from Lesson 6 in class or at home and revise as necessary.
- Have students share their revisions in groups or have volunteers write their old and new sentences on the board.

Lesson 8 | What do you think?

page 51

Giving feedback

- Tell students that they are going to read four other students' paragraphs and that they will need a sheet of paper for Exercise 4.

1
- Read the instructions for Exercise 1 aloud, including the chart.
- Have students in one group of four exchange paragraphs with another group of four.
- Have students read all four of the other group's paragraphs. They can take turns reading them aloud one by one, or read them silently and pass them around the group.
- Give students time to discuss and complete the chart.
- Walk around the classroom, helping students as necessary.

2
- Read the instructions for Exercise 2 aloud.
- Have each student choose just one paragraph to use for Exercises 2, 3, 4, and 5.
- Have students complete Exercise 2 individually.

3
- Read the instructions for Exercise 3 aloud.
- Call on students to read the sentences in Exercise 3.
- Have students complete the exercise individually.
- When they finish, tell them to exchange books and review their partner's answers. They can then go on to Exercise 4.

4
- Read the instructions for Exercise 4 aloud. Then call on a student to read the example letter.
- Have students write their letters to their partner individually.
- Walk around the classroom, helping students as necessary.

5

- Read the instructions for Exercise 5 aloud.
- Have students give their letters to their partner. Give them time to tell their partner the answer to the question in the letter.

- Have students revise their paragraphs based on the comments they receive and other ideas they have. They can complete their revisions either in class or at home.
- Have students turn in their revised paragraphs to you.

| Option | Group flag |

page 52   **Just for fun**

- If you can, provide students with poster paper, markers or colored pencils, colored paper, scissors, and glue. You can also bring in old magazines for students to cut up for pictures.
- Encourage students to be creative!

1

- Read the instructions for Exercise 1 aloud.
- Have students work in small groups to choose a club or class as the subject for their flag.

2

- Read the instructions for Exercise 2 aloud.
- Read the words in the Word File aloud and have the class repeat. Explain vocabulary as necessary.
- Have students work in groups to complete the exercise. They can all work together on each symbol, or have two students work on one symbol and two students work on the other.
- Walk around the classroom, helping students as necessary.

3

- Read the instructions for Exercise 3 aloud.
- Have students work with their groups to complete the exercise. Remind groups to let all members participate equally.

4

- Read the instructions for Exercise 4 aloud.
- Suggest ways that groups can work together to complete the poster (e.g., different students can be in charge of drawing, coloring, writing, or directing the work).
- Give students time to plan their work.
- Have students work in groups to complete their posters.
- If necessary, write these phrases on the board so groups can borrow materials from each other:

  May I borrow the (tape)?

  Can I use the (blue marker)?

  Sure, go ahead.

  I'm sorry, we're still using it.
- Walk around the classroom, helping students as necessary.

5

- Read the instructions for Exercise 5 aloud.
- Groups can take turns explaining different parts, or select one member to make the presentation.
- After the presentations, hang the posters around the classroom.

 Unit **6** *It's a party!*

Overview

In this unit, students plan a class party. They write a notice and a paragraph describing their party plans, with details about time, place, and activities. They also learn to plan a paragraph by making a list.

The prewriting lessons focus on brainstorming details about the party and organizing them in a clear and logical way. The main writing assignment in Lesson 6 shows students how to combine a notice and a paragraph into one piece of writing. The postwriting lesson shows students how to add an explanation to a suggestion by using *so that* and *to* to combine two sentences. The *Option: Just for fun* lesson teaches students some basic principles of graphic design as they create posters for their parties.

	Lesson	Focus	Estimated Time
1	Class activities	Brainstorming	10–20 minutes
2	Let's go on a hike!	Analyzing sentences	10–20 minutes
3	Class party!	Prewriting	15–25 minutes
4	Plans and instructions	Learning about organization	10–20 minutes
5	Planning a paragraph	Learning about organization	20–30 minutes
6	My party	Writing	30–40 minutes
7	*So that* and *to*	Editing	15–25 minutes
8	What do you think?	Giving feedback	20–30 minutes
	Party poster design	Option: Just for fun	30–40 minutes

Key points

➤ Encourage students to give sufficient details in their party plans. Remind them that anything they don't mention in their notices and paragraphs can't be carried out.

➤ After the party plans are finished, we suggest voting on one as a class to actually hold. You should set any limitations and requirements for the party (such as when and where the party could take place) in advance.

➤ For the *Option: Just for fun* lesson, bring or ask students to bring sheets of poster paper, colored pencils and markers, old magazines to cut up, scissors, tape, and glue.

➤ Useful language for this unit includes imperatives, *going to* and *will*, and *let's*.

➤ Sections can be skipped. A minimal set of lessons might include 3, 4, 5, and 6.

page 53

Brainstorming

1
- Read the instructions for Exercise 1 aloud.
- Call on students to read the caption for each of the pictures. Explain vocabulary as necessary.
- Have students complete Exercise 1 individually.
- Go over responses as a whole class by reading each activity aloud and having students raise their hands if they would like to do the activity with the class.

2
- Read the instructions for Exercise 2 aloud.
- Have students complete the exercise individually. Set a time limit of five minutes.
- Walk around the classroom, helping students as necessary.

3
- Read the instructions for Exercise 3 aloud.
- Have students compare lists with a partner and add more ideas to their own lists.
- Call on some students to read their list of ideas aloud to the class or write them on the board.

Optional activity

Brainstorming activities for other occasions
Write other occasions relevant to your students' lives on the board (e.g., graduation or birthday party). Have students work in groups to brainstorm activities for these occasions. Set a time limit of five to eight minutes. Ask groups to write their three best ideas on the board. Then have the class vote on the three best ideas overall.

page 54

Analyzing sentences

1
- Read the instructions for Exercise 1 aloud.
- Ask students to tell you what they see in the picture. Provide vocabulary as necessary.
- Have students read the paragraph individually.
- Call on students to read the paragraph aloud, sentence by sentence. Point out the exclamation point, used here to mark exciting information.
- Read the instructions for a–d aloud.
- Have students complete a–d individually.
- If your students are having difficulty, you may want to stop after 1b and review.
- Ask students to raise their hands or nod to let you know when they have finished.

2
- Have students compare answers with a partner.
- Go over answers as a whole class. Call on students to write the sentences for 1c–d on the board. Check punctuation.

Answers
1. **a.** a class hike
   b. Don't forget to bring a water bottle. We'll meet at Bell School at 6:50 a.m.
   c. Winter is coming, so let's go on a class ski trip!
   d. Bring a coat and gloves because it will probably be cold.

Optional activity

What do we need?
With the class, brainstorm possible activities for a class trip (e.g., a hike, a trip to the beach, a camping trip). Divide the class into small groups and have each group brainstorm items they will need for one of the trips. Have them work together to write sentences like this: Summer is coming, so let's go to the beach! Bring a big hat because the sun is strong. When they finish, have one student from each group read their sentences to the class. Can the class think of anything they forgot to mention?

Lesson 3 — Class party!

Prewriting

page 55

1

- Read the instructions for Exercise 1 aloud.
- Call on a student to read the information in the notice aloud. Explain vocabulary as necessary.
- Have students complete Exercise 1 individually.
- Go over answers as a whole class.

Answers
Date: June 1
Starting time: 11:00 a.m.
Cost per person: Free
Contact person: Andy
Location: English class
Ending time: 12:10 p.m.

2

- Read the instructions for Exercise 2 aloud.
- Have students complete Exercise 2 individually. Encourage them to write about a party they really want to have, since these notes will be used for the main writing assignment.

- Walk around the classroom, helping students as necessary.
- Have students compare ideas with a partner.

3

- Read the instructions for Exercise 3 aloud. Remind students that a topic sentence gives general information about the paragraph.
- Call on a student to read the examples.
- Have students complete Exercise 3 individually.
- Call on some students to write their topic sentences on the board. Walk around the classroom to check the other students' sentences.

Lesson 4 — Plans and instructions

Learning about organization

page 56

- Read the information at the top of page 56.
- Call on students to read the example plans and instructions.
- Point out that the plans use *will* and the instructions use the imperative.

1

- Read the instructions for Exercise 1 aloud.
- Ask students to tell you what they see in the pictures. Provide vocabulary as necessary.
- Have students complete Exercise 1 individually. Point out that they should use the pictures to suggest what words to write.
- Walk around the classroom, helping students as necessary.
- Have students compare answers with a partner. Point out that all of the sentences are plans.

Answers
1. a. Bell School
  b. bus
  c. hike / walk
  d. eat lunch / have a picnic

2

- Read the instructions for Exercise 2 and the Word File aloud.
- Have students complete the exercise individually.
- Have students compare answers with a partner. Point out that all of the sentences are instructions.

39

Lesson 5 — Planning a paragraph

Learning about organization

page 57

■ Read the top of page 57 aloud.

1

■ Read the instructions for Exercise 1 aloud.

■ Call on students to read the sample lists aloud. Explain vocabulary as necessary.

■ Have students work alone to complete the exercise.

■ Walk around the classroom, helping students as necessary.

2

■ Read the instructions for Exercise 2 aloud.

■ Have students complete the exercise individually. Set a time limit of five to seven minutes.

■ Ask the class, *How is this kind of list like a brainstorm?* (Answer: It's like a brainstorm because you write words and phrases instead of sentences and because you will get ideas from which you can write a well-organized paragraph.)

3

■ Have students show their lists to a partner. Encourage them to explain why they did or didn't check each item.

■ Give students time to revise their lists as necessary. Remind them that the ideas they check will be the ones they include in their paragraphs.

Lesson 6 — My party

Writing

pages 58–59

1

■ Read the instructions for Exercise 1 aloud.

■ Have students read the paragraph individually.

■ Call on students to read the paragraph aloud. Explain vocabulary as necessary.

■ Read the instructions for a–d aloud.

■ Have students complete a–d individually or with a partner.

■ Go over answers as a whole class.

2

- Read the instructions for Exercises 2 and a–b aloud, including *Write these things* and the cues that follow.
- Have students complete the exercises individually.
- Walk around the classroom, helping students as necessary.

3

- Read the instructions for Exercise 3 aloud.
- Have students write their notice and paragraph on lined paper or type it. Have them skip lines. Tell them you'll collect the paragraphs after they're revised in Lessons 7 and 8.

- Have students complete Exercise 3 either at home or in class.

In your journal . . .

- *If time permits, read the journal entry instructions aloud. Tell students to write as many details about the party as they can.*
- *Students can write in class or at home.*

Lesson 7	*So that* and *to*

page 60 **Editing**

- Read the top of page 60 aloud.
- Call on a student to read the examples.
- Point out that in sentences like these, *so that* is followed by a subject and a verb, while *to* is followed immediately by a verb.
- Point out that here, *so that* and *to* mean the same thing. Encourage students to use both forms in their writing to make it more interesting.

I

- Read the instructions for Exercise 1 aloud.
- Read sentences a–f aloud. Explain vocabulary as necessary.
- Have students work with a partner to complete the exercise. They should discuss the answers together.
- Go over answers as a whole class.

Answers

I. a. I will go to the restaurant tomorrow **so that** I can make reservations for our party.

I will go to the restaurant tomorrow **to** make reservations for our party.

b. Let's swap lunches on Tuesday **so that** we can see what other people like to eat.

Let's swap lunches on Tuesday **to** see what other people like to eat.

c. I think we should go to the movie early **so that** we can buy popcorn and drinks for everyone.

I think we should go to the movie early **to** buy popcorn and drinks for everyone.

d. Please bring a hat **so that** you can keep from getting a sunburn.

Please bring a hat **to** keep from getting a sunburn.

e. Let's meet at 6:15 **so that** we can get to the concert before it starts.

Let's meet at 6:15 **to** get to the concert before it starts.

f. Bring some money **so that** you can rent a boat at the lake.

Bring some money **to** rent a boat at the lake.

2

- Read the instructions for Exercise 2 aloud.
- Have students check their paragraphs from Lesson 6 in class or at home and revise as necessary.
- Have students share their revisions in groups or have volunteers write their old and new sentences on the board.

page 61
Giving feedback

■ Tell students that they are going to read each other's paragraphs and that they will need a sheet of paper for Exercise 2.

1

■ Read the instructions for Exercises 1 and a–b aloud.

■ Have students exchange their paragraphs with a partner and complete Exercises a–b individually.

■ Ask the class, *In 1b, how many people circled "fun"? "unique"?* Ask how many people wrote their own ideas to describe their partner's party, and what they were.

■ Tell students to exchange books and review their partner's answers.

2

■ Read the instructions for Exercise 2 aloud. Then call on a student to read the example letter.

■ Have students write their letters to their partner individually.

■ Walk around the classroom, helping students as necessary.

3

■ Read the instructions for Exercise 3 aloud.

■ Give students time to walk around, look at the party ideas, and choose the ones they like best.

■ Walk around the classroom with your students and make a list of the party ideas. Write the list on the board.

4

■ Read the instructions for Exercise 4 aloud.

■ Read the party ideas that you wrote on the board one at a time. Students raise their hands if they chose the idea as one of their three favorites. Tally the results to see which party is the class favorite.

Optional activity

Party committees

If you are going to actually hold a class party, divide the class into committees. Each committee should be responsible for one aspect of the party as outlined in the party plans (e.g., food, music, clean up, etc.). Have them plan what they will do for the party and then present their plans to the rest of the class, who can point out anything they forgot. Then, enjoy the party!

Option   **Party poster design**

page 62
Just for fun

■ Bring or ask students to bring materials such as markers or colored pencils, poster paper, magazines to cut up for pictures, stickers, scissors, glue, and tape to create a poster.

1

■ Read the instructions for Exercises 1 and 1a aloud.

■ Read the words in the box aloud and have students repeat. Explain vocabulary as necessary.

■ Read the instructions for Exercise 1b aloud, including the design ideas. Explain vocabulary as necessary.

■ Have students complete Exercises a–b individually.

2

■ Read the instructions for Exercise 2 aloud.

■ Have students complete their posters individually.

■ Walk around the classroom, helping students as necessary.

■ If necessary, write these phrases on the board so groups can borrow materials from each other:

May I borrow the (tape)?

Can I use the (blue marker)?

Sure, go ahead.

I'm sorry, I'm still using it.

■ Students can finish their posters at home as necessary.

3

■ Read the instructions for Exercise 3 aloud.

■ Hang the posters around the room, and let students walk around to look at them and decide which ones they would like to attend. They do not need to choose the same parties they did in Lesson 8.

Unit 7 *Thank-you letter*

Overview

In this unit, students write a thank-you letter to someone expressing appreciation. They also learn how to give reasons and use time markers such as *before*, *while*, and *after*.

In the prewriting lessons, students learn different expressions to show their appreciation. They learn to support their points with specific examples and to order the events of a story in chronological order. The central writing assignment of the unit in Lesson 6 reviews the format for a letter. In the postwriting lesson, students learn to shift clauses that begin with *after* and *before* to make their writing more interesting. The *Option: Just for fun* lesson shows students how to expand the skills they learned in the unit to write a letter of appreciation to a company or business.

	Lesson	Focus	Estimated Time
1	Things to be thankful for	Brainstorming	15–25 minutes
2	A thank-you letter	Analyzing sentences	10–20 minutes
3	Giving reasons II	Learning about organization	20–30 minutes
4	Someone to thank	Prewriting	15–25 minutes
5	Time markers	Learning about organization	15–25 minutes
6	Thank you	Writing	30–40 minutes
7	*Before* and *after*	Editing	15–25 minutes
8	What do you think?	Giving feedback	20–30 minutes
	A company I appreciate	Option: Just for fun	20–30 minutes

Key points

➤ Students can sometimes become emotional when writing or listening to classmates' personal letters.

➤ Encourage students to give their final thank-you letters to the people they wrote them to, and if possible, have them report on the recipients' reactions.

➤ Students are introduced to basic elements related to narrative writing. Encourage students to relay important details so that their classmates can get a clear picture of the event they're describing.

➤ Useful language for this unit includes expressions of thanks and appreciation; *Thank you for _____ing*; and *before, while,* and *after*.

➤ Sections can be skipped. A minimal set of lessons might include 3, 4, 5, and 6.

Things to be thankful for

page 63

Brainstorming

1

- Read the instructions for Exercise 1 aloud.
- Ask students to tell you what they see in the pictures. Provide vocabulary as necessary.
- Have a student read the examples aloud.
- Have students complete Exercise 1 individually.
- Go over responses with the whole class by reading each example aloud and having students raise their hands if they checked it.

2

- Read the instructions for Exercise 2 aloud.
- Have students complete the exercise individually. Set a time limit of five minutes.

- Walk around the classroom, helping students as necessary. They may ask you for some new vocabulary words.

3

- Read the instructions for Exercise 3 aloud.
- Have students compare lists with a partner and add more ideas to their own lists.
- Call on some students to read their list of ideas aloud to the class or write them on the board.

Lesson 2
A thank-you letter

page 64

Analyzing sentences

- Ask students to brainstorm about gifts they've received. They can write a list on paper or just think.

1

- Read the instructions for Exercise 1 aloud.
- Have students read the paragraph individually.
- Call on students to read the paragraph aloud, sentence by sentence. Explain vocabulary as necessary.
- Read the instructions for a–d aloud.
- Have students complete a–d individually.
- Walk around the classroom, encouraging and helping students as necessary.
- If your students are having difficulty, you may want to stop after 1b and review.
- Ask students to raise their hands or nod at you to let you know when they have finished.

2

- Have students compare answers with a partner.
- Go over answers as a whole class. Have students write the answers for 1c–d on the board.

Answers
1. a. I am writing to thank you for the lovely gift.
   b. am sometimes late, just the right size for my desk.
   c. I am writing to thank you for taking me to the concert.
   d. Thanks so much again for the thoughtful gift.

Optional activity

Thank-you cards

Tell students that in English-speaking countries, it's customary for people to send thank-you cards after they've received birthday or holiday gifts. (If you have any samples, bring them to class.) Tell students that they are going to write a thank-you card for a gift they recently received. Have students work in groups and discuss gifts that they have recently received. They should say what the gift was and why they were thankful for it. They can use the language modeled in the paragraph on page 64. Then, using similar language, they should write thank-you cards. Suggest they send their cards to the gift givers.

Lesson 3	Giving reasons II

page 65 — **Learning about organization**

- Read the top of page 65 aloud.
- Have students read the examples on the top of the page.

1

- Read the instructions for Exercise 1 and sentences a–c aloud. Explain vocabulary as necessary.
- Have students work with a partner to complete the exercise.
- Walk around the classroom, helping students as necessary.
- Go over answers as a whole class by calling on students to read the sentences aloud or write them on the board.

Answers

1. a. I want to thank you for giving me a birthday party.

b. I want to thank you for showing me where the library is.

c. I want to thank you for saving me a seat in the cafeteria.

2

- Read the instructions for Exercise 2 aloud.
- Have students complete Exercise 2 individually.
- If some students are having difficulty, elicit examples from other students to demonstrate.
- Walk around the classroom, helping students as necessary.

3

- Read the instructions for Exercise 3 aloud.
- If possible, have the students arrange their chairs in a circle, so they can see everybody.
- Call on a student to start the chain.
- If you notice that not everyone is being thanked, encourage students to spontaneously make up a thank-you sentence for the students who have not been thanked yet, or create a sentence yourself thanking those students. Everyone should get a turn to thank and be thanked.

Lesson 4	Someone to thank

page 66 — **Prewriting**

1

- Read the instructions for Exercise 1 aloud.
- Call on a student to read the examples.
- Have students complete the chart individually.
- Walk around the classroom, helping students as necessary and checking their work.

2

- Read the instructions for Exercise 2 aloud.
- Have students work with a partner to complete the exercise.

Optional activity

Extension of Exercise 2

Write the questions for Exercise 2 on the board, or ask students to memorize them. Have students close their books and stand up. When you say "Go," students approach a classmate and ask the questions. Set a time limit of two minutes, and then have them move on to another classmate. Continue the game for 10–12 minutes or until students are tired. Then ask the class, What was the most surprising thing someone was thankful for? What was the nicest thing you heard? If students got more ideas after this exercise, give them time to add them to their brainstorming lists from Lesson 1.

3

- Read the instructions for Exercise 3 aloud. Note that now they are going from talking about someone in the third person (*he* or *she*) to the second person (*you*).

- Have students complete the exercise in class or at home.
- Walk around the classroom, helping students as necessary.
- Go over answers as a whole class or have students compare answers with a partner.

| Lesson 5 | **Time markers** |

page 67 **Learning about organization**

- Read the information at the top of page 67 aloud.
- Ask students to tell you what they see in the pictures. Provide vocabulary as necessary.
- Read the first example sentence aloud while students look at the picture. Ask students which event happened first. (Answer: My friends brought a cake to my house and put up a sign.)
- Read the second example sentence aloud while students look at the picture. Point out that the two events happened at the same time.
- Read the third example sentence aloud while students look at the picture. Ask students which event happened first. (Answer: I came in and turned on the light.)

1

- Read the instructions for Exercise 1 aloud.
- Read the paragraph aloud, skipping the blanks. Explain vocabulary as necessary.
- Have students complete Exercise 1 individually.
- Have students compare answers with a partner.
- Go over the answers as a whole class.

Answers

1. One evening **after** school, I walked to the bus stop. **While** I was walking, it started to rain, but I did not have an umbrella. **While** I was waiting for the bus, I got wetter and wetter. About ten minutes **before** the bus came, an old man walked up to the bus stop. He saw how wet I was, so he took off his jacket and gave it to me **while** we were talking. Even today, **after** so many years, I am still grateful to that man for his kindness.

2

- Read the instructions for Exercise 2 aloud.
- Have students complete the exercise individually, either in class or at home.
- Have students compare sentences with a partner.
- Call on some students to write their sentences on the board. Walk around the classroom to check the other students' sentences.

| Lesson 6 | **Thank you** |

pages 68–69 **Writing**

1

- Read the instructions for Exercise 1 aloud.
- Have students read the letter individually.
- Call on students to read the letter aloud, sentence by sentence. Explain vocabulary as necessary.
- Read the instructions for a–c aloud.
- Have students complete a–c individually or with a partner.
- Go over answers as a whole class.

Answers

1. a. I'm writing to thank you for helping me at school one day.
　　b. Before, While, After
　　c. Best regards; Yours truly

2

- Read the instructions for Exercise 2 aloud, including *Write these things* and the cues that follow.

46

- Have students complete the exercise individually.
- Walk around the classroom, helping students as necessary.

3

- Have students write their letter on lined paper or type it. Have them skip lines. Tell them you'll collect the letters after they're revised in Lessons 7 and 8.

In your journal . . .

- *If time permits, read the journal entry instructions aloud. Tell students they can also write about different ideas related to the nice thing they did. Ask them to use the time markers* before, while, *and* after *if they can.*
- *Students can write in class or at home.*

Lesson 7	*Before and after*

page 70 **Editing**

- Read the top of page 70 aloud.
- Read the examples aloud. When you read the sentences that begin with *Before* and *After*, pause after the first clause to show where the comma should go.

1

- Read the instructions for Exercise 1 aloud.
- Call on a student to read the first example.
- Have students work with a partner to complete the exercise. Remind students that they can use *before* and *after* at the beginning of some sentences and in the middle of others. Remind them to use commas correctly.
- Students who finish early or higher-level students can write each item both ways (with *before* or *after* at the beginning and in the middle).
- Go over answers as a whole class.

Answers

Sentences will vary. Possible answers:

1. 2 I was happy.

  1 You took me to a movie.

    I was happy after you took me to a movie.

    After you took me to a movie, I was happy.

  1 I got your advice.

  2 I felt better.

    I felt better after I got your advice.

    After I got your advice, I felt better.

---

2 You gave me a gift.

1 I didn't know how kind you were.

  I didn't know how kind you were before you gave me a gift.

  Before you gave me a gift, I didn't know how kind you were.

2 I listened to your advice.

1 I did not know how to solve my problem.

  I did not know how to solve my problem before I listened to your advice.

  Before I listened to your advice, I did not know how to solve my problem.

1 You heard that I was in the hospital.

2 You called me.

  You called me after you heard that I was in the hospital.

  After you heard that I was in the hospital, you called me.

2

- Read the instructions for Exercise 2 aloud.
- Have students who want to change the order of clauses in their paragraphs from Lesson 6 revise at home.
- Have students share their revisions in groups or have volunteers write their old and new sentences on the board.

Lesson 8 — What do you think?

page 71

Giving feedback

- Tell students that they are going to read each other's thank-you letter paragraphs and that they will need a sheet of paper for Exercise 2.

1
- Read the instructions for Exercises 1 and a–b aloud.
- Have students exchange their paragraphs with a partner and complete Exercises a–b individually. Walk around the classroom, helping students as necessary.
- Tell students to exchange books and review their partner's answers.

2
- Read the instructions for Exercise 2 aloud. Then call on a student to read the example letter.

- Have students write their letters to their partner individually.
- Walk around the classroom, helping students as necessary.

3
- Read the instructions for Exercise 3 aloud.
- Have students give their letters to their partner. Give them time to tell their partner the answer to the question in the letter.

- Have students revise their paragraphs based on the comments they receive and other ideas they have. They can complete their revisions either in class or at home.
- Have students turn in their revised paragraphs to you.

Option — A company I appreciate

page 72

Just for fun

- Start by asking students if they've ever used a product or received a service that they really liked. Tell them that they will have a chance to thank a company for a product or service they appreciate.

1
- Read the instructions for Exercise 1 aloud.
- Call on students to read the captions below the illustrations.

2
- Read the instructions for Exercises 2 and a–b aloud.
- Have students complete a–b individually.
- You may have to help students choose a company. If necessary, have the class brainstorm some examples and write them on the board.
- If your students do not have Internet access, have them use companies whose address they can find in the phone book, or let them invent addresses.

3
- Read the instructions for Exercise 3 aloud.
- Have students complete their letters individually, either in class or at home. Have them type their letters if possible.
- Have students compare their letters in groups.
- If possible, check the letters for accuracy, and then have your students send them. Tell them to report back to the class if they get a response.

Overview

In this unit, students write a review of a movie, including a summary and their opinion of the movie. They also learn how to write a two-paragraph composition.

In the prewriting lessons, students write about the characters, actors, plot, and message of a movie. They support their opinion of the movie with details and examples. In Lesson 6, students organize their ideas into two paragraphs, with a topic sentence for each one. They end the second paragraph with a general conclusion. In the postwriting editing lesson, students learn to avoid repetition of names by using pronouns. In the *Option: Just for fun* lesson, students work in groups to create a story for a movie, design a poster to advertise it, and hold a mock press conference.

	Lesson	Focus	Estimated Time
1	Great movies	Brainstorming	10–20 minutes
2	Parts of a movie review	Analyzing sentences	10–20 minutes
3	Movie summaries	Learning about organization	20–30 minutes
4	Writing more than one paragraph	Learning about organization	20–30 minutes
5	Movie interview	Prewriting	20–30 minutes
6	My movie review	Writing	30–40 minutes
7	Pronouns	Editing	20–30 minutes
8	What do you think?	Giving feedback	20–30 minutes
	The movie producers	Option: Just for fun	30–40 minutes

Key points

➤ From this unit on, students will write two paragraphs instead of one. More emphasis should be placed on teaching expository organization, such as putting different topics in separate paragraphs and clearly marking paragraph topics with topic sentences.

➤ Guide students in their movie choices so that they do not all choose the same movies and so they choose movies with plots and messages that are easy to write about.

➤ You might have one or two students who rarely watch movies. Let them write book reviews instead.

➤ Useful language for this unit includes present and past verb tenses, adjectives to describe movies, and pronouns.

➤ Sections can be skipped. A minimal set of lessons might include 3, 4, 5, and 6.

Brainstorming

page 73

- You might want to start this unit with a brief class discussion about movies. Ask students what kinds of movies they like.

1

- Read the instructions for Exercise 1 aloud.
- Ask students to tell you what they see in the pictures. Provide vocabulary as necessary.
- Read the movie titles in a–f aloud and have students repeat.
- Have students work with a partner to complete the exercise.
- Have students check their answers at the bottom of the page.
- Ask the class, *How many people have seen* Titanic? The Lord of the Rings? *etc.*, and have students raise their hands. Call on a few students to give their opinions of the movies.

Answers
1. a. 3
   b. 2
   c. 1
   d. 5
   e. 6
   f. 4

2

- Read the instructions for Exercise 2 aloud.

Note: *Explain to students that italics, a style of writing that slants to the right, is used to denote movie titles in printed material. Tell them that <u>underlining</u> represents italics in handwritten form.*

- Have students complete the exercise individually. Set a time limit of five minutes.
- Walk around the classroom, helping students as necessary. They may ask you for some new vocabulary words related to titles. They may also write movie titles in their own language if necessary.

3

- Read the instructions for Exercise 3 aloud.
- Have students compare lists with a partner and add more ideas to their own lists.
- Call on some students to read their list of ideas aloud to the class or write them on the board.

Analyzing sentences

page 74

1

- Read the instructions for Exercise 1 aloud.
- Have students read the paragraph individually. Provide vocabulary as necessary.
- Call on students to read the paragraph aloud, sentence by sentence. Explain vocabulary as necessary.
- Read the instructions for a–d aloud.
- Have students answer a–d individually.
- If your students are having a difficult time, you may want to stop after 1b and review.
- Ask students to raise their hands or nod at you to let you know when they have finished.

2

- Have students compare their answers with a partner.

- Go over answers as a whole class. If any students have seen the movies mentioned, ask them if they agree with the main message.

Answers
1. a. characters: ★ little boy, ★ psychologist
      actors: ★★ Haley Joel Osment,
      ★★ Bruce Willis
   b. that ghosts are not always bad
   c. (The movie) <u>Master and Commander</u> is about an English captain who fights a French ship.
   d. The main message of <u>Star Wars</u> is that the good side wins.

page 75

Learning about organization

- Tell students that movie summaries like the ones they will write give readers the most important information about the movie.
- Read the top of page 75 aloud.
- Write the following on the board:
  the characters and actors
  the plot
  the message
- Elicit definitions from the students and write them on the board:
  the characters and actors: *people in a movie; stars of a movie*
  the plot: *what happens in the movie; the story*
  the message: *what the movie is trying to tell or teach the audience*

- Read the instructions for Exercise 1 aloud.
- Give students a minute or so to choose a movie and write it down.
- You may want to ask students to share what movies they've chosen.

2

- Read the instructions for Exercise 2 aloud.
- Have students read the three movie reviews individually.
- Call on students to read the three movie reviews aloud. Explain vocabulary as necessary.
- Read the instructions for a–c aloud.
- Have students complete a–c individually.
- Have students compare responses with a partner. Walk around while students are talking to check their work.

Optional activity

The sequel
Ask students if they know what a sequel is. If not, explain that it is a movie that is a continuation of a first movie. Give some examples (e.g., the Star Wars movies, the Harry Potter movies, the Matrix movies). Have students work in small groups. Each group should pick a movie that doesn't already have a sequel. They should discuss an idea for a sequel and then write a summary of the sequel, including the information modeled in Lesson 3. When they are finished, have them present their summaries to the class.

page 76

Learning about organization

- Ask students how they decide whether or not they should go to a movie. Elicit answers (e.g., from advertisements, from a friend's recommendation, because popular stars are in it). Tell them that many people decide to see a movie based on a movie review, which is what they will read and write in this unit.
- Read the top of page 76. Explain vocabulary as necessary.

- Read the instructions for Exercise 1 aloud.
- Have students read the paragraph individually.
- Call on students to read the paragraph aloud, sentence by sentence. Explain vocabulary as necessary.

- Tell students that the second paragraph begins when the main topic changes.
- Have students complete Exercise 1 individually.
- Go over answers with the whole class. Ask them to tell you the topic of the first paragraph (summary of the movie) and the second paragraph (the writer's opinion of the movie).

Answer
1. Bend It Like Beckham was very entertaining.

2

- Read the instructions for Exercise 2 aloud.
- Have students work with a partner to complete the exercise.

51

- Go over answers as a whole class.
- Ask if any students have seen this movie. If they have, elicit their opinions about it.

> **Answers**
> **2. a.** 1
>   **b.** 2
>   **c.** 2
>   **d.** 1

3

- Read the instructions for Exercise 3 and the words in the box aloud. Explain vocabulary as necessary.
- Have students complete the exercise individually.
- Walk around the classroom, helping students as necessary. They may ask you for some vocabulary.
- Have students compare answers with a partner or in small groups.
- Ask who wrote their own words. Write the new words on the board for the whole class.

Lesson 5	Movie interview

Prewriting

page 77

1

- Read the instructions for Exercise 1 aloud.
- Read the instructions for a–b aloud, including the questions. Have students suggest additional questions and write them on the board.
- Have students work with a partner to complete the exercise.
- Walk around the classroom, helping students as necessary.

2

- Read the instructions for Exercise 2 aloud.
- Have a student read the example aloud. Point out that the last sentence contains the recommendation.
- Have students complete Exercise 2 individually.

- Have students compare responses with a partner. Walk around the classroom, helping students as necessary and checking their work.

> **Optional activity**
>
> *Talk show: movie review*
> *Have students work together with a partner to practice a talk show in which they review a movie. Each student gives his or her opinion of the movie, supported by reasons. The students do not have to agree with each other. Have them create a rating system for each movie (one to four stars, or one or two thumbs up). Give each pair a few minutes to present their talk show to the class.*

Lesson 6	My movie review

Writing

page 78

1

- Read the instructions for Exercise 1 aloud.
- Ask students to tell you what they see in the picture. Does anyone know what movie Jun's thinking about?
- Have students read the paragraphs individually.
- Call on students to read the paragraphs aloud. Explain vocabulary as necessary.
- Read the instructions for a–c aloud.

- Have students complete a–c individually or with a partner.
- Go over answers as a whole class.

> **Answers**
> **1. a.** <u>Titanic</u> is a movie about a ship that sinks. I think <u>Titanic</u> was a great movie.
>   **b.** Jack and Rose
>   **c.** Love is strong and everlasting.

2

- Read the instructions for Exercise 2 aloud, including *Remember to write* and the cues that follow.

- Have students write their paragraphs on lined paper or type them. Have them skip lines. Tell them you'll collect the paragraphs after they're revised in Lessons 7 and 8.

In your journal . . .

- *If time permits, read the journal entry instructions aloud. Tell students they can also write about their favorite and least favorite actors.*

- *Students can write in class or at home.*

| Lesson 7 | **Pronouns** |

page 79

- Read the information on the top of page 79 aloud.
- Call on students to read the examples aloud.
- Explain that students should avoid repeating names too much because it becomes boring.
- Students do not need to learn the names of the different types of pronouns.

1

- Read the instructions for Exercise 1 aloud.
- Have students complete the exercise individually. Point out that Harry and Ron are boys and that Hermione is a girl.
- If students are having difficulty, tell them there are fourteen changes to be made (not including the example).
- Have students compare answers with a partner.
- Go over answers as a whole class. Point out that not every name can be replaced by a pronoun, because the text would be confusing.

Answers

1.   One message of the Harry Potter movies is that good friends are important. Harry has many problems in **his** life. **He**

is always in danger. However, Harry solves **his** problems because **he** has some good friends to help **him**. **They** are not typical kids. **They** know magic and have some special skills. Harry's best friend is Ron. **He** is loyal and dependable. **He** often helps Harry get out of danger. Harry's other good friend is Hermione. **She** is very smart and good at **her** studies. Hermione helps Harry with **his** homework. Harry depends a lot on Ron and Hermione, and **they** help **him** through many adventures. **Their** friendship is one of my favorite things about the movies.

2

- Read the instructions for Exercise 2 aloud.
- Have students who want to change names to pronouns in their paragraphs from Lesson 6 revise them at home.
- Have students share their revisions in groups or have volunteers write their old and new sentences on the board.

| Lesson 8 | **What do you think?** |

Giving feedback

page 80

- Tell students that they are going to read one another's reviews and that they will need a sheet of paper for Exercise 4.

1

- Read the instructions for Exercise 1 aloud.
- Have students sit with their groups and take turns reading another group's reviews.

2

- Read the instructions for Exercise 2 aloud. Explain vocabulary as necessary.
- Have students work with their groups to complete Exercise 2.
- Ask the class if anyone created their own award category. Write any new categories on the board.

3

- Read the instructions for Exercise 3 aloud.
- Have students complete the exercise individually.
- Walk around the classroom, helping students as necessary.
- Tell students to exchange books and review their partner's answers.

4

- Read the instructions for Exercise 4 aloud. Then call on a student to read the example letter.
- Have students write their letters to their partner individually.
- Walk around the classroom, helping students as necessary.

5

- Read the instructions for Exercise 5 aloud. Have students give their letters to their partner. Give them time to tell their partner the answer to the question in the letter.

6

- Read the instructions for Exercise 6 aloud.
- Have the groups take turns presenting the awards.
- Ask students if they agree with the award their movie won.

- Have students revise their paragraphs based on the comments they receive and other ideas they have. They can complete their revisions either in class or at home.
- Have students turn in their revised paragraphs to you.

Option	**The movie producers**

page 81 **Just for fun**

- Students will need large pieces of paper or poster board and colored pencils or markers.

1

- Read the instructions for Exercise 1 aloud.
- Have students work in groups to decide on a movie name. Set a time limit of three to five minutes.

2

- Read the instructions for Exercise 2 aloud.
- Students can discuss their ideas and have one person write them down, or write their ideas individually and then discuss them. Set a time limit of 15 minutes.

3

- Read the instructions for Exercise 3 aloud.
- Have students work in their groups to complete the exercise. Have them use the names of real actors.

4

- Read the instructions for Exercise 4 and the example movie poster aloud. Point out that the poster shows the movie title, the actors, the characters, and the plot.
- Have students work in their groups to complete Exercise 4.
- Walk around the classroom, helping students as necessary.

5

- Read the instructions for Exercises 5 and a–b aloud.
- Have students complete the exercise with the same group they worked with in Exercises 1–4. Encourage students to be dramatic and have fun.
- If time permits, have each group present their press conference and poster to the class.
- Display the posters around the classroom.

Unit **9** *Friendship*

Overview

In this unit, students write about a friend. They also learn to write supporting sentences.

In the prewriting lessons, students learn vocabulary for describing people and brainstorm qualities of a good friend. They strengthen their opinions by writing supporting sentences that give examples. In Lesson 6, students write two paragraphs about their friend. In the first paragraph, they describe the qualities that make the person a good friend. In the second paragraph, they write about something they would like to do for their friend. In the postwriting editing lesson, students learn to connect result clauses with a main sentence by using *so*. In the *Option: Just for fun* lesson, students interview a classmate and write a magazine article based on the interesting information they discover.

	Lesson	Focus	Estimated Time
1	Qualities of a friend	Brainstorming	15–25 minutes
2	A good friend	Analyzing sentences	10–20 minutes
3	Friendship Quiz	Prewriting	15–25 minutes
4	Supporting sentences	Learning about organization	20–30 minutes
5	Something special for a friend	Prewriting	20–30 minutes
6	My friend	Writing	30–40 minutes
7	Combining sentences with *so*	Editing	15–25 minutes
8	What do you think?	Giving feedback	20–30 minutes
	People magazine	Option: Just for fun	30–40 minutes

Key points

➤ Encourage students to choose a friend that has admirable personal qualities that they can support with examples. The friend could also be a family member.

➤ The final task in this unit could be to give the paragraphs to the person written about, which you might want to explain early in the unit. If possible, have students report on the recipients' reactions.

➤ Useful language includes vocabulary to describe people and personalities; *will* and *would like*; and *so* to connect sentences.

➤ Sections can be skipped. A minimal set of lessons might include 4, 5, and 6.

page 82

Brainstorming

I

- Read the instructions for Exercise 1 aloud. Tell students that for this exercise, they should think about friends in general, not a specific person.

- Read the words in the box and have the class repeat. Then read sentences a–f, skipping the blanks. Explain vocabulary as necessary.

- Have students work with a partner to complete the exercise.

- Go over answers as a whole class.

Answers

I. a. kind

  b. funny

  c. dependable

  d. honest

  e. generous

  f. loyal

2

- Read the instructions for Exercise 2 aloud. Tell students they should now think of specific people.

- Have students work alone to complete the exercise. Set a time limit of five minutes.

- Walk around the classroom, helping students as necessary.

3

- Read the instructions for Exercise 3 aloud.

- Have students compare lists with a partner and add more ideas to their own lists.

- Call on some students to read their list of ideas aloud to the class or write them on the board.

---

page 83

Analyzing sentences

I

- Read the instructions for Exercise 1 aloud.

- Have students read the paragraph individually.

- Call on students to read the paragraph aloud, sentence by sentence. Explain vocabulary as necessary.

- Read the instructions for a–d aloud.

- Have students complete a–d individually.

- If students are having difficulty, you may want to stop after 1b and review.

- Ask students to raise their hands or nod at you to let you know when they have finished.

2

- Have students work with a partner to compare their answers.

- Go over answers as a whole class.

- Have students write the answers to 1c–d on the board.

Answers

I. a. dependable, honest, funny

  b. (She is) there whenever I need someone to talk to; (she) always tells me the truth; (if I am sad, Lisa) makes me feel better with her jokes.

  c. Bill is my best friend.

  d. Bill is cheerful and generous.

Optional activity

A friend is someone who is . . .

Have students work individually to complete this sentence with one or two adjectives. They can look up words in their dictionaries or ask you for help. Have students write their sentences on the board. How many students chose the same qualities?

page 84

Prewriting

1

- Read the instructions for Exercise 1 aloud.
- Read each of the quiz sentences aloud. Explain vocabulary as necessary.
- Have students complete the quiz individually. Point out that the answers are the students' own opinions. There are no "right" answers.
- Go over responses as a whole class by reading each sentence aloud and asking, *How many people ranked this with three or four stars? with one or two stars?* Have students raise their hands to show their responses.

2

- Read the instructions for Exercise 2 aloud.
- Have students complete the exercise individually.
- Walk around the classroom, helping students as necessary.
- Have students compare answers with a partner or group.

Lesson 4   Supporting sentences

Learning about organization

page 85

- Read the top of page 85 aloud.
- Call on a student to read the examples.
- Point out that supporting sentences make statements easier to understand by giving more specific information.

1

- Read the instructions for Exercise 1 aloud. Point out that these sentences are not about the person they chose in Lesson 3, Exercise 2.
- Have students complete the exercise individually.
- Have students compare their responses with a partner or a group.

2

- Read the instructions for Exercise 2 aloud.

- Have students complete the exercise individually.
- Walk around the classroom, helping students as necessary.
- Go over responses as a whole class. Call on students to read their sentences aloud or write them on the board.

Optional activity

Additional support

Write several of the adjectives from Lessons 1 and 3 on the board. Have students work with a partner. Assign the same one or two adjectives to two pairs. Tell them to write three or more supporting sentences to explain the adjective(s). Then have the pairs compare their sentences.

Lesson 5   Something special for a friend

Prewriting

page 86

1

- Read the instructions for Exercise 1 aloud.
- Call on students to read the examples in the pictures.
- Have students complete Exercise 1 individually.
- Go over responses as a whole class by asking students to read their responses aloud.

2

- Read the instructions for Exercise 2 aloud.
- Call on a student to read the example aloud. Explain vocabulary as necessary.

- Have students complete Exercise 2 individually. Encourage them to make plans that they could realistically carry out.
- Walk around the classroom, helping students as necessary.

3

- Have students compare their charts with a partner. Tell students that they may make additions to their original chart.

Lesson 6 — My friend

page 87

Writing

- Read the instructions for Exercise 1 aloud.
- Have students read the paragraphs individually.
- Call on students to read the paragraphs aloud. Explain vocabulary as necessary.
- Read the instructions for a–d aloud. Point out that before students underline the topic sentence in 1a, they should determine what the topic of the paragraph is.
- Have students complete a–d individually or with a partner.
- Go over answers as a whole class.

> **Answers**
> **1. a.** Carla from Brazil is one of my best friends.
>
> **b.** honest, dependable, trustworthy
>
> **c.** She is honest because she always tells me the truth about everything – even about how I look. She is dependable because she always does what she says she is going to do. Finally, Carla is

trustworthy because she never tells anyone the secrets I tell her.

d. I think it will be a lonely time for her, so I would like to invite her to come and stay at my house with my family.

2

- Read the instructions for Exercise 2 aloud, including *Remember to write* and the cues that follow.
- Have students write their paragraphs on lined paper or type them. Have them skip lines. Tell them you'll collect the paragraphs after they're revised in Lessons 7 and 8.

> **In your journal . . .**
>
> - *If time permits, read the journal entry instructions aloud. Tell students that they can also write about the kind of friend they would like to be, using the structure would like to explain their ideas.*
> - *Students can write in class or at home.*

Lesson 7 — Combining sentences with *so*

page 88

Editing

- Read the instructions at the top of page 88 aloud.
- Call on a student to read the examples. Point out that a comma precedes the clause that begins with *so*.
- Ask students to look back at the second paragraph in Lesson 6, Exercise 1, and underline the sentence connected with *so* (Answer: I think it will be a lonely time for her, so I would like to invite her to come and stay at my house with my family).

- Read the instructions for Exercise 1 aloud.
- Call on a student to read 1a aloud.
- Have students work with a partner to complete the exercise. Make sure they identify the result before writing the new sentence.

- Walk around the classroom, helping students as necessary.
- Go over answers as a whole class.

> **Answers**
> **1. a.** result: I want to take him to a soccer game.
>
> Naoki loves soccer, so I want to take him to a soccer game.
>
> **b.** result: I know I can trust her.
>
> Laura never tells secrets, so I know I can trust her.
>
> **c.** result: She knows a lot about me.
>
> I have known Sasha since we were six, so she knows a lot about me.

d. result: I am lonely.

My best friend moved away, so I am lonely.

e. result: I can always ask him for help.

Paul is kind, so I can always ask him for help.

f. result: I will lend him some money.

Ryan needs to buy a new soccer ball, so I will lend him some money.

g. result: She always makes me laugh.

My friend tells great jokes, so she always makes me laugh.

h. result: I will buy him some new software.

My best friend loves video games, so I will buy him some new software.

2

■ Read the instructions for Exercise 2 aloud.

■ Have students who want to combine sentences revise their paragraphs from Lesson 6 at home.

■ Have students share their revisions in groups, or have volunteers write their old and new sentences on the board.

Lesson 8	**What do you think?**

page 89 **Giving feedback**

■ Tell students that they are going to read each other's paragraphs and that they will need a sheet of paper for Exercise 2.

1

■ Read the instructions for Exercises 1 and a–d aloud.

■ Have students exchange their paragraphs with a partner and complete a–d individually. Walk around the classroom, helping students as necessary.

■ When they finish, ask the class, *In 1d, how many people checked (fun)?* See which was the most popular adjective chosen. Ask how many people wrote their own ideas and what they were.

■ Tell students to exchange books and review their partner's answers.

2

■ Read the instructions for Exercise 2 aloud. Then call on a student to read the example letter.

■ Have students write their letters to their partner individually.

■ Walk around the classroom, helping students as necessary.

3

■ Read the instructions for Exercise 3 aloud.

■ Have students give their letters to their partner. Give them time to tell their partner the answer to the question in the letter.

■ Have students revise their paragraphs based on the comments they receive and other ideas they have. They can complete their revisions either in class or at home.

■ Have students turn in their revised paragraphs to you.

page 90

■ Ask students if they've ever read magazine articles about people. Ask, *Where have you read these articles? What makes them interesting?*

1

■ Read the instructions for Exercise 1 aloud.

■ Ask students to tell you what they see in the picture. Provide vocabulary as necessary.

■ Have students read the paragraph individually.

■ Call on students to read the paragraph aloud, sentence by sentence. Explain vocabulary as necessary.

2

■ Read the instructions for Exercise 2 and the words from the box aloud.

■ Have the class brainstorm some examples of questions on each topic and write them on the board.

■ Have students work with a partner to interview each other. Set a time limit of seven to ten minutes.

■ Walk around the classroom, helping students as necessary.

3

■ Read the instructions for Exercise 3 aloud.

■ Have students complete the exercise individually.

4

■ Read the instructions for Exercise 4 aloud.

■ Have students complete their articles individually, in class or at home.

■ Have students exchange their articles with their partner. Give them time to discuss the articles and make changes, if necessary.

■ Walk around the classroom, helping students as necessary and checking their work.

5

■ Read the instructions for Exercise 5 aloud.

■ Call on students to give some possible titles for their articles.

■ You may wish to have students type or write their articles neatly so you can put them into a class magazine.

6

■ Read the instructions for Exercise 6 aloud.

■ Have students draw their partner or collect a photo. A digital picture could be used if the student typed the article.

■ If possible, compile everyone's articles and photos and put a magazine together for the class. Students can then sign it or write special messages by their pictures or on the covers.

Overview

In this unit, students write about a superhero power they would like to have, such as the ability to travel through time. They also learn how to write about situations that are not real.

In the prewriting lessons, students make wishes about superhero powers they would like to have and discuss with classmates what those wishes might mean. They learn to logically connect problems with imaginary solutions. In Lesson 6, they write one paragraph about a specific problem they have and a superhero power that would solve it and a second paragraph about what they would do with that power. In the postwriting editing lesson, they practice structures for expressing wishes. The *Option: Just for fun* lesson lets students work with a partner to create a comic strip, combining art with their writing.

	Lesson	Focus	Estimated Time
1	Mightyman	Brainstorming	15–25 minutes
2	Becoming a superhero	Analyzing sentences	10–20 minutes
3	Expressing wishes I	Prewriting	20–30 minutes
4	Choosing superhero powers	Prewriting	20–30 minutes
5	Situations that aren't real	Learning about organization	15–25 minutes
6	My superhero power	Writing	30–40 minutes
7	Expressing wishes II	Editing	15–25 minutes
8	What do you think?	Giving feedback	20–30 minutes
	Comic book	Option: Just for fun	30–40 minutes

Key points

➤ This unit brings out students' imaginations and creativity. Brainstorm some popular superheroes with your class to set the mood. Bring to class examples of comic books or short video clips if possible.

➤ Make sure students come up with a specific problem the superpower would allow them to solve. They do not need to choose a significant or deeply personal problem. Students can choose an ordinary situation such as not wanting to ride a crowded bus, which could be solved by being able to fly.

➤ Useful language for this unit includes *I wish I could . . .* ; *If I could . . . , I would . . .* ; and *If I were . . .*

➤ Sections can be skipped. A minimal set of lessons might include 3, 4, 5, and 6.

61

page 91

Brainstorming

1

■ Read the instructions for Exercise 1 and the phrases in the box aloud. Explain vocabulary as necessary.

■ Ask students to tell you what they see in the pictures. Provide vocabulary if necessary.

■ Have students work with a partner to complete Exercise 1.

■ Go over answers with the whole class.

■ Ask students if they know of a superhero similar to Mightyman.

> **Answers**
> **1. a.** speak ten languages
>
> **b.** become invisible
>
> **c.** fly
>
> **d.** see through walls
>
> **e.** stop a train
>
> **f.** read minds

2

■ Read the instructions for Exercise 2 aloud.

■ Have students complete the exercise individually. Set a time limit of five minutes.

■ Walk around the classroom, helping students as necessary.

3

■ Read the instructions for Exercise 3 aloud.

■ Have students compare lists with a partner and add more ideas to their own lists.

■ Call on some students to read their list of ideas aloud to the class or write them on the board.

> **Optional activity**
>
> **Who's your favorite superhero? What can he or she do?**
> Have students work alone to write about their favorite superhero (now or when they were a child) and what the superhero can do. After five minutes, have students work in groups and share their information. If time permits, call on students one at a time to name their favorite superheroes. Write the names on the board. Who is the class favorite? What can he or she do?

Lesson 2 | **Becoming a superhero**

page 92

Analyzing sentences

1

■ Read the instructions for Exercise 1 aloud.

■ Ask students to tell you what they see in the picture. Provide vocabulary as necessary.

■ Have students read the paragraph individually.

■ Call on students to read the paragraph aloud, sentence by sentence.

■ Read the instructions for a–d aloud.

■ Have students answer a–d individually.

■ If your students are having a difficult time, you may want to stop after 1b and review.

■ Ask students to raise their hands or nod at you to let you know when they have finished.

2

■ Have students compare answers with a partner.

■ Go over answers as a whole class. Call on students to write answers to 1c–d on the board. Check punctuation.

> **Answers**
> **1. a.** I am often late for work because of traffic jams.
>
> **b.** explains how to solve a problem
>
> **c.** I wish I could see the future.
>
> **d.** If I could see the future, I would invest money in stocks.

page 93

Prewriting

1

- Read the instructions for Exercise 1 aloud.
- Call on students to read the captions under the pictures. Explain vocabulary as necessary.
- Have students complete the exercise individually.
- Walk around the classroom, helping students as necessary.
- Go over answers as a whole class.

Answers
1. **a.** I wish I could fly.
   b. I wish I could see through walls.
   c. I wish I could travel through time.
   d. I wish I could read minds.
   e. I wish I could become invisible.
   f. I wish I could breathe underwater.

2

- Read the instructions for Exercise 2 aloud. Tell students that they will be taking a kind of psychology test to see what their wishes mean.
- Have students work with a partner to complete the exercise.
- Walk around the classroom, helping students as necessary. Explain vocabulary as necessary.
- Go over responses as a whole class. You might want to make a class chart to find out which was the most popular superhero power. Ask students if they thought their partner's interpretation was correct.

page 94

Prewriting

1

- Read the instructions for Exercise 1 aloud.
- Call on a student to read the thought bubbles aloud.
- Have students work with a partner to complete the exercise.
- Go over answers as a whole class.

Answers
1. **a.** 2
   b. 3
   c. 1
   d. 1
   e. 2
   f. 3

2

- Read the instructions for Exercise 2 aloud.
- Have a student read the examples.
- Have students complete the exercise individually.
- Walk around the classroom, helping students as necessary.

3

- Read the instructions for Exercise 3 aloud.
- Have students complete the exercise with their partner.
- Go over responses as a whole class. Call on some students to tell the class what powers they chose and what problems they can solve.

page 95

Learning about organization

- Read the top of page 95 aloud.
- Have a student read the example sentences aloud.
- Point out the placement of the comma after *If I could . . .*
- Ask students how many of them would like to communicate with their pets or other animals.

- Read the instructions for Exercise 1 aloud.
- Have students complete Exercise 1 individually.
- Go over answers as a whole class. Call on students to write the sentences on the board. Check punctuation.

Answers

1. a. If I could talk to animals, I would communicate with Ginger, my dog.

b. If I could talk to animals, I would ask her what kind of food she likes.

c. If I could talk to animals, I would ask her why she's afraid of the vacuum cleaner.

d. If I could talk to animals, I would teach her how to use the TV.

2

- Read the instructions for Exercise 2 aloud.
- Have students complete Exercise 2 individually. Point out that they are writing notes, not complete sentences.
- Walk around the classroom, helping students as necessary. They may ask you for some vocabulary.

3

- Read the instructions for Exercise 3 aloud.
- Have students complete the exercise individually.
- Have students compare answers with a partner.
- Go over answers as a whole class. Write or have students write several examples on the board.

Optional activity

If you could see the future

Tell students that they have been granted the power to see the future, but that they can only do one thing with this special power. Give students a few minutes to write sentences about what thing they will choose to see and why. Then have students stand up and share their sentences with as many other students as possible in ten minutes. After time is up, ask students about the choices they heard from their classmates. This game can also be played by asking students to pretend they could change one event in the past.

---

pages 96–97

Writing

1

- Read the instructions for Exercise 1 aloud.
- Have students read the paragraphs individually.
- Call on students to read the paragraphs aloud, sentence by sentence. Explain vocabulary as necessary.
- Read the instructions for a–c aloud.
- Have students complete a–c individually or with a partner.
- Go over answers as a whole class.

Answers

1. a. I love Ginger, my dog, but we cannot communicate very well.

If I could talk to animals, I would ask Ginger many questions and teach her useful things.

---

b. ask Ginger many questions, teach her useful things, ask her what kind of food she likes, (ask her) why she is afraid of the vacuum cleaner, teach her how to use the TV, tell her about the girl that I like, ask Ginger's advice

c. Paragraph 1: It explains a way to solve a problem.

Paragraph 2: It explains why the superhero power would be important to Jamie.

2 _____

■ Read the instructions for Exercises 2 and a–b, including the cues that follow.

Lesson 7	Expressing wishes II

■ Read the top of page 98 aloud.

■ Call on students to read the examples aloud.

■ Point out that these are all different ways to express wishes. Point out the structure, *I wish I were.* Tell students that people sometimes say *I wish I was* but use the more traditional *I wish I were* in writing. Point out that *want* will always be followed by *to.*

■ Ask students to look at the paragraphs in Lesson 6, Exercise 1, and underline any sentences with *want to* or *wish* (Answer: I would like to be able to communicate more with Ginger, so I wish I could talk to animals). Ask them to notice how every sentence in paragraph 2 uses *If I/we could . . .* or *I/we would . . .*

1 _____

■ Read the instructions for Exercise 1 aloud. Explain that in some cultures, people write their wishes on slips of paper and tie them to the branches of a tree.

Lesson 8	What do you think?

■ Tell students that they are going to read each other's paragraphs and that they will need a sheet of paper for Exercise 2.

■ Have students complete the exercises individually.

■ Walk around the classroom, helping students as necessary.

3 _____

■ Have students write their paragraphs on lined paper or type them. Have them skip lines. Tell them you'll collect the paragraphs after they're revised in Lessons 7 and 8.

In your journal . . .

■ *If time permits, read the journal entry instructions aloud. Tell students that they can also write about their current favorite superhero or fictional character.*

■ *Students can write in class or at home.*

---

page 98   **Editing**

■ Have students complete Exercise 1 individually.

■ Have students compare answers with a partner.

■ Go over answers as a whole class.

Answers
1. a. could, would
   b. were, want
   c. want, could
   d. were, could or would

---

2 _____

■ Read the instructions for Exercise 2 aloud.

■ Have students check their paragraphs from Lesson 6 in class or at home and revise as necessary.

■ Have students share their revisions in groups, or have volunteers write their old and new sentences on the board.

---

page 99   **Giving feedback**

1 _____

■ Read the instructions for Exercises 1 and 1a aloud.

■ Have students exchange their paragraphs with a classmate and complete Exercise 1a individually.

■ Read the instructions for b–c aloud.

- Have students work in groups of four. The people they exchanged paragraphs with should not be in their groups.

- Have students take turns telling the group about the paragraphs they read.

- Have students complete b–c in their groups. Walk around the classroom, helping students as necessary.

- When they finish, ask the class, *In 1b, what was the "best superhero power" you chose?* Also see which was the most unusual, funniest, and most practical superhero power chosen. Ask how many people wrote their own ideas, and what they were.

2 ———————————————

- Read the instructions for Exercise 2 aloud.

- Call on a student to read the example letter aloud.

- Have students write their letters to their partner from Exercise 1a individually.

- Walk around the classroom, helping students as necessary.

3 ———————————————

- Read the instructions for Exercise 3 aloud.

- Have students give their letters to their partner. Give them time to tell their partner the answer to the question in the letter.

———————————————

- Have students revise their paragraphs based on the comments they receive and other ideas they have. They can complete their revisions either in class or at home.

- Have students turn in their revised paragraphs to you.

Option	**Comic book**

page 100   **Just for fun**

- Bring or have students bring markers or colored pencils to class.

- Students can also write and design their comic on a computer, if they wish.

- Ask the class to tell you what comic books they know. If any students are current comic book fans, let the rest of the class ask them some questions about their interests.

1 ———————————————

- Read the instructions for Exercises 1 and a–c aloud.

- Have a student read the sample comic aloud. Explain vocabulary as necessary.

- Have students work with a partner to complete a–c.

- Have students discuss their ideas with a partner.

2 ———————————————

- Read the instructions for Exercise 2 aloud.

- Call on students to read the example story notes.

- Have students work with a partner to complete Exercise 2. They should discuss their ideas, choose a story together, and then write notes.

3 ———————————————

- Read the instructions for Exercise 3 aloud.

- Call on students to read the comic captions and dialogue.

- Have students work with a partner to complete the exercise. They can take turns writing and drawing, or one student can write and the other one draw.

- If some students want to draw very detailed comics, have them complete their work at home.

- Display all the comics on a large table or post them around the room, so everyone can read them.

Unit 11 Advertisements

Overview

In this unit, students write a magazine advertisement for a product. They also learn how to write advertising language.

In the prewriting lessons, students write claims about what a product can do. They learn techniques for catching the reader's attention in the first few lines of a paragraph, and they learn how to end the paragraph with a recommendation to the buyer. In Lesson 6, students write a one-paragraph testimonial from someone who has used the product and a second paragraph describing what the product is and what it can do. In the postwriting editing lesson, students practice using superlatives to describe their products. The *Option: Just for fun* lesson has students recycle the advertising language they practiced as they set up a mock flea market.

	Lesson	Focus	Estimated Time
1	Products and advertising claims	Brainstorming	10–20 minutes
2	An advertisement	Analyzing sentences	10–20 minutes
3	Claims and recommendations	Learning about organization	15–25 minutes
4	Attention getters	Learning about organization	15–25 minutes
5	Writing a testimonial	Prewriting	20–30 minutes
6	My advertisement	Writing	25–35 minutes
7	Using persuasive language	Editing	15–25 minutes
8	What do you think?	Giving feedback	20–30 minutes
	Flea market	Option: Just for fun	30–40 minutes

Key points

➤ Try to begin the unit with a TV commercial or magazine advertisement to help set the scene. Make sure the advertisement has a user testimonial.

➤ Tell students whether they should write advertisements about realistic or fanciful products (such as "self-folding clothes"). Lessons 1–3 display realistic products, while Lessons 4–6 focus on fanciful products.

➤ To focus on real-world application, you can have your students write advertisements for products related to their field of work or interest. Students might also write advertisements for local merchants.

➤ Useful language for this unit includes imperatives and superlative adjectives.

➤ Sections can be skipped. A minimal set of lessons might include 3, 4, 5, and 6.

Lesson 1   Products and advertising claims

page 101

Brainstorming

- Ask students where they see advertisements (magazines, billboards, subways, etc.). Ask them what their favorite advertisements are.

1

- Read the instructions for Exercise 1 aloud.
- Ask students to tell you what they see in the pictures. Provide vocabulary as necessary.
- Call on students to read the advertising claims.
- Have students work with a partner to complete the exercise.
- Go over answers as a whole class.

> **Answers**
> **1. a.** 3
>   **b.** 4

c. 2
d. 1

2

- Read the instructions for Exercise 2 aloud.
- Have students complete the exercise individually. Set a time limit of five minutes.
- Walk around the classroom, helping students as necessary. They may ask you for some new vocabulary words.

3

- Read the instructions for Exercise 3 aloud.
- Have students compare lists with a partner and add more ideas to their own lists.
- Call on some students to read their list of ideas aloud to the class or write them on the board.

Lesson 2   An advertisement

page 102

Analyzing sentences

1

- Read the instructions for Exercises 1 and a–d aloud.
- Ask students to tell you what they see in the picture.
- Have students read the paragraph individually.
- Call on students to read the paragraph aloud, sentence by sentence. Explain vocabulary as necessary.
- Have students complete a–d individually.
- If your students are having a difficult time, you may want to stop after 1b and review.
- Ask students to raise their hands or nod at you to let you know when they have finished.

2

- Have students compare answers with a partner.
- Go over answers as a whole class. Have students write the answers for 1c–d on the board.

> **Answers**
> **1. a.** comfortable, attractive
>   **b.** (you'll) run faster and jump higher, (your) friends will envy you
>   **c.** Lightning Coffee is the strongest and most powerful coffee ever made.
>   **d.** If you drink this coffee, you'll be able to study all day and all night.

Optional activity

Analyzing real advertisements

Bring in or have students bring in advertisements from newspapers or magazines. Have students work in groups, and give each group several advertisements to look at. They should go over each advertisement, choose a favorite, and write a short description telling what the product is and what it does. Collect the descriptions and the advertisements. Post the advertisements around the room and read the descriptions aloud. Have the class point to the one that is being described.

page 103

Learning about organization

■ Write the words *advertising claim* and *advertising recommendation* on the board and ask students if they know what the words mean.

■ Read the information at the top of page 103 aloud.

1

■ Read the instructions for Exercise 1 aloud.

■ Read sentences a–d aloud. Explain vocabulary as necessary.

■ Have students work with a partner to complete the exercise.

■ Walk around the classroom, helping students as necessary.

■ Go over answers as a whole class. Have students write the answers on the board.

■ Point out the comma after the *if*-clause.

Answers
1. a. You will run faster and jump higher.

b. You will quench your thirst.

c. You will have a beautiful smile.

d. You will feel stronger and look younger.

a. If you wear these sneakers, you will run faster and jump higher.

b. If you drink it when it's hot outside, you will quench your thirst.

---

c. If you use it every morning and evening after meals, you will have a beautiful smile.

d. If you take one every morning at breakfast, you will feel stronger and look younger.

2

■ Read the instructions for Exercise 2 and the example aloud.

■ Have students complete the exercise individually.

■ Walk around the classroom, helping students as necessary.

■ Elicit responses from the class and write some examples on the board.

3

■ Read the instructions for Exercise 3 and the Word File aloud.

■ Have students complete the exercise individually.

■ Go over answers as a whole class.

Answers
3. a. Try

b. See

c. Come

d. Buy

---

page 104

Learning about organization

■ Read the top of page 104 aloud.

■ Call on a student to read the examples of attention getters.

1

■ Read the instructions for Exercise 1 aloud.

■ Ask students to tell you what they see in the pictures. Provide vocabulary as necessary.

■ Have students work individually to complete the exercises.

■ Go over answers as a whole class.

■ Ask the class, *Which attention getters are sentences?* (Answers: a and d) *Which attention getter is a question?* (Answer: c) *Which are surprising or funny?* (Answers: a, c, and d) *Which are about problems you have?* (Answers: b and c)

2

- Read the instructions for Exercise 2 aloud.
- Have students complete the exercise individually.
- Have students compare responses with a partner.
- Go over responses as a whole class. Write some examples on the board.

Lesson 5	Writing a testimonial

Prewriting

page 105

- Ask students if they know what the word *testimonial* means.
- Read the top of page 105 aloud.
- Call on a student to read the examples.
- Ask students if they can remember any advertising testimonials from print, television, or radio advertisements. Write some examples on the board.

1

- Read the instructions for Exercise 1 aloud.
- Call on students to read the examples. Explain vocabulary as necessary.

- Have students complete Exercise 1 individually.
- Walk around the classroom, helping students as necessary.

2

- Read the instructions for Exercise 2 aloud.
- Have students work with a partner to complete the exercise.
- Call on students to read their testimonials to the class. Encourage them to be dramatic.

Lesson 6	My advertisement

Writing

pages 106–107

1

- Read the instructions for Exercise 1 aloud.
- Have students read the testimonial and advertisement individually.
- Call on students to read the testimonial and advertisement aloud, sentence by sentence. Explain vocabulary as necessary.
- Read the instructions for a–b aloud.
- Have students complete a–b individually or with a partner.
- Go over answers as a whole class.

2

- Read the instructions for Exercises 2 and a–b, including the cues that follow.
- Have students complete the exercise individually.
- Walk around the classroom, helping students as necessary.

3

- Have students write their testimonial and advertisement on lined paper or type them. Have them skip lines. Tell students to include a drawing or photo of the customer or product. Tell them you'll collect the paragraphs after they're revised in Lessons 7 and 8.

In your journal . . .

- *If time permits, read the journal entry instructions aloud. Tell students that they can also write about favorite advertisements and their claims and recommendations. They can also write about why they like or dislike advertisements.*
- *Students can write in class or at home.*

Lesson 7 — Using persuasive language

Editing

page 108

- Read the top of page 108 aloud.
- Call on students to read the examples aloud.
- Ask students to look back at the paragraph in Lesson 2, Exercise 1, and underline the superlatives (Answer: most comfortable and attractive).

d. most powerful (loudest)
e. loudest (most powerful), smoothest
f. smartest

1

- Read the instructions for Exercise 1 aloud.
- Have students complete Exercise 1 individually.
- If students are having difficulty, first have them write the superlative form of the adjectives in the box and check answers. Then have them complete the sentences.
- Have students compare answers with a partner.
- Go over answers as a whole class.

Answers
1. a. scariest
  b. biggest
  c. funniest

2

- Read the instructions for Exercise 2 aloud.
- Have students who want to add superlatives revise their paragraphs from Lesson 6 at home.
- Have students share their revisions in groups, or have volunteers write their old and new sentences on the board.

Optional activity

Superlative practice
Have students work with a partner or in small groups. Tell them to brainstorm a list of adjectives and then write their superlative form. Compare adjective lists as a class.

Lesson 8 — What do you think?

Giving feedback

page 109

- Tell students that they are going to read each other's advertisements and that they will need a sheet of paper for Exercise 2.

1

- Read the instructions for Exercises 1 and a–b aloud.
- Have students work in groups of three and exchange their advertisements with another group.

71

- Have students work in groups to complete a–b.

- Walk around the classroom, helping students as necessary.

- When they finish, ask the class, *In 1a, how many people chose (fashionable)?* See which was the most popular product description chosen. Ask how many people wrote their own ideas, and what they were.

2

- Read the instructions for Exercise 2a aloud.

- Have students choose an advertisement and then complete Exercise 2a individually.

- Tell students to exchange books and review their partner's answers.

- Read the instructions for Exercise 2b aloud. Then call on a student to read the example letter aloud.

- Have students complete Exercise 2b individually.

- Walk around the classroom, helping students as necessary.

- Read the instructions for Exercise 2c aloud.

- Have students give their letters to their partner. Give them time to tell their partner the answer to the question in the letter.

- Have students revise their advertisements based on the comments they receive and other ideas they have. They can complete their revisions either in class or at home.

- Have students turn in their revised paragraphs to you.

Optional activity

Acting it out

Have students work in small groups. Have them read each member's advertisement and then choose one to act out as a short television commercial. Encourage them to be persuasive and to have fun with it. They can add to the ideas the author originally wrote if they wish. Have all the groups perform for the class.

| Option | **Flea market** |

Just for fun

- Ask students if they've ever heard of a flea market. Tell them that it is an open-air market where people sell used items. Tell students that they'll be creating a flea market in the classroom.

- If you wish, have students add prices to their items and pretend to sell them.

1

- Read the instructions for Exercise 1 aloud.

- Have students complete the exercise individually. Make sure they are describing objects they have with them to display.

- Walk around the classroom, helping students as necessary.

2

- Read the instructions for Exercise 2 aloud.

- Have students complete the exercise individually.

- Walk around the classroom, helping students as necessary.

3

- Read the instructions for Exercise 3 aloud.

- Arrange the classroom for the flea market. Spread items and descriptions on a few large tables, or have students push a row of desks together to serve as display tables.

- Have half of the students display their items while the other half of the class walks around the room to look at all the items and ask questions. Then have the two groups switch roles.

- Encourage students to be convincing salespeople!

Overview

In this final unit, students write about an action they regret. They also learn to write a concluding paragraph.

In the prewriting lessons, students practice describing situations and learn to describe the consequences of an action by adding explanations and drawing conclusions. In Lesson 6, students write one paragraph explaining the mistake and the damage it did and a second paragraph explaining what they learned from the experience. In the postwriting editing lesson, students vary word choice by replacing common adjectives with more descriptive synonyms. In the *Option: Just for fun* lesson, students write a poem about the action they regret and make a sympathy or apology card from it.

	Lesson	Focus	Estimated Time
1	Regrets	Brainstorming	10–20 minutes
2	A regret	Analyzing sentences	10–20 minutes
3	Writing an explanation	Learning about organization	15–25 minutes
4	Something I regret	Prewriting	15–25 minutes
5	Conclusions	Learning about organization	20–30 minutes
6	My regret	Writing	30–40 minutes
7	Word choice	Editing	15–25 minutes
8	What do you think?	Giving feedback	20–30 minutes
	Make a card	Option: Just for fun	20–30 minutes

Key points

➤ Since students are reflecting on and assessing negative past actions, this unit has the potential to become emotional. When students share their papers, remind them not to be critical or judgmental of their classmates.

➤ The unit combines many of the skills and techniques students have learned in previous units, such as using topic sentences, using transition words, explaining cause and effect, and writing narratives.

➤ Useful language for this unit includes past tense verbs and adjectives to describe feelings.

➤ Sections can be skipped. A minimal set of lessons might include 3, 4, 5, and 6.

Lesson 1 Regrets

page 111

Brainstorming

■ Ask students if they know the word *regret*. If they don't, have them work with a partner to look it up in the dictionary and share an explanation of the noun and verb with the class.

1

■ Read the instructions for Exercise 1 aloud.

■ Ask students to tell you what they see in the pictures. Provide vocabulary as necessary.

■ Call on a student to read the captions under each picture.

■ Have students work individually to complete the exercise.

■ Have students compare responses with a partner.

2

■ Read the instructions for Exercise 2 aloud.

■ Have students work individually to complete the exercise. Set a time limit of five minutes.

■ Walk around the classroom, helping students as necessary.

3

■ Read the instructions for Exercise 3 aloud.

■ Have students compare lists with a partner and add more ideas to their own lists.

■ Call on some students to read their list of ideas aloud to the class or write them on the board.

Optional activity

Class pet peeves

Write *pet peeve* on the board. Explain to students that a pet peeve *is something that another person does that bothers them a lot (e.g., being late, telling lies, or borrowing money). Give students a few minutes to write some of their pet peeves individually. Tell them not to write about specific people. Then have students stand and talk to their classmates about what three things bother them most about other people. Call on students to tell the class some of the things they learned about their classmates.*

Lesson 2 A regret

page 112

Analyzing sentences

1

■ Read the instructions for Exercise 1 aloud.

■ Ask students to tell you what they see in the picture.

■ Have students read the paragraph individually.

■ Call on students to read the paragraph aloud, sentence by sentence. Explain vocabulary as necessary.

■ Read the instructions for a–d aloud.

■ Have students complete a–d individually.

■ If your students are having difficulty, you may want to stop after 1b and review.

■ Ask students to raise their hands or nod at you to let you know when they have finished.

2

■ Have students compare answers with a partner.

■ Go over answers as a whole class. Have students write the answers to c–d on the board.

Answers

1. a. I've learned that I should tell the truth.

   b. angry, guilty

   c. I will always feel bad about stealing my brother's book.

   d. He was angry, so I said I was sorry and gave it back.

74

page 113 **Learning about organization**

■ Read the information on the top of page 113. Explain vocabulary as necessary.

■ Call on students to read the examples.

1

■ Read the instructions for Exercise 1 aloud.

■ Have students work with a partner to complete the exercise.

■ Go over answers as a whole class.

d. I promised I would never lie to her again. She forgave me, but I still can't go out for a month!

Answers

1. a. She was sad. I said I was sorry, and I'm going to take her to the movies tonight.

b. I didn't have enough money, so I could not pay him back.

c. My little brother brought his friends into my bedroom to play.

Optional activity

Judge and jury

Brainstorm a list of about five mistakes similar to the examples in Lesson 3 and write them on the board. Then, in small groups, have students work together to write the following: 1) what the consequences should be; and 2) how the situation could be fixed. Put two groups together and have them read their ideas to each other, or have each group read their ideas to the whole class.

page 114 **Prewriting**

1

■ Read the instructions for Exercise 1 aloud.

■ Have students complete the exercise individually. They can use an idea from Lesson 1 or think of a new idea.

■ Have students compare responses with a partner.

■ Call on some students to share their responses with the class.

2

■ Read the instructions for Exercise 2 aloud.

■ Call on a student to read *The situation* and *What I did wrong* aloud. Ask students to guess how Jenny felt. Then call on a student to read *The consequences* aloud.

■ Have students complete the exercise individually. Remind students that the consequences could be their feelings, the other person's feelings, or some events.

■ Walk around the classroom, helping students as necessary.

3

■ Have students compare responses in groups of three.

■ Call on some students to share their responses with the class.

■ Give students time to add ideas or information to their charts.

■ Read the information at the top of page 115 aloud.

1

■ Read the instructions for Exercise 1 aloud.

■ Call on a student to read the example.

■ Have students complete the exercise individually.

■ Go over the answer as a whole class.

Answer

1. I should ask permission before I borrow things.

2

■ Read the instructions for Exercise 2 aloud.

■ Have students work with a partner to complete the exercise.

■ Go over answers as a whole class.

Answers

Answers will vary. Possible answers:

2. a. I should allow more time to get to work in case of traffic.

b. I shouldn't lend my homework to anyone.

---

c. I shouldn't lie because then people won't trust me.

d. I should always take responsibility for my actions.

3

■ Read the instructions for Exercise 3 aloud.

■ Have students complete the exercise individually.

■ Call on some students to share their responses with the class.

Optional activity

Stories with morals

Find two or three short stories with a moral, such as stories from Aesop's Fables, in the library or on the Internet and read them to the class. Read one with its moral to the class. Then read a second one, but don't read the moral. Have students work in groups to write their idea of what the moral is. Have groups read their ideas to the class.

1

■ Read the instructions for Exercise 1 aloud.

■ Have students read the paragraphs individually.

■ Call on students to read the paragraphs aloud, sentence by sentence. Explain vocabulary as necessary.

■ Read the instructions for a–d aloud.

■ Have students complete a–d individually or with a partner.

■ Go over answers as a whole class.

Answers

1. a. Something I will always feel sorry about is losing my friend Ashley's scarf.

That experience taught me two things.

b. 1. I borrowed a scarf.

2. I promised to be careful with it.

3. I left it on the train.

4. I apologized.

5. Ashley didn't get angry.

---

c. guilty, sad, angry

d. I must be more careful with other people's things.

Ashley taught me what true friendship is.

2

■ Read the instructions for Exercise 2 aloud, including *Remember to write* and the cues that follow.

■ Have students write their paragraphs on lined paper or type them. Have them skip lines. Tell them you'll collect the paragraphs after they're revised in Lessons 7 and 8.

| Lesson 7 | **Word choice** |

■ Read the information at the top of page 117 aloud.

■ Call on students to read the examples.

■ Remind students to use a variety of vocabulary to make their writing more interesting.

1

■ Read the instructions for Exercise 1 aloud.

■ Call on a student to read the words in the box. Explain vocabulary as necessary.

■ Have students complete the exercise individually.

■ Have students compare answers with a partner.

■ Go over answers as a whole class.

> **Answers**
> **1.** Good feelings: excited, proud, relieved
>
> Bad feelings: angry, ashamed, depressed, disappointed, embarrassed

2

■ Read the instructions for Exercise 2 aloud.

■ Have students complete the exercise individually.

■ Walk around the classroom, helping students as necessary.

> **In your journal . . .**

> ■ *If time permits, read the journal entry instructions aloud. Tell students to try to use vocabulary and expressions from the unit.*
>
> ■ *Students can write in class or at home.*

page 117   Editing

■ Have students compare answers with a partner. Encourage them to discuss differences of opinion.

■ Go over answers as a whole class.

> **Answers**
> **2. a.** excited, angry
>   **b.** relieved
>   **c.** depressed
>   **d.** disappointed
>   **e.** embarrassed
>   **f.** ashamed, proud

3

■ Read the instructions for Exercise 3 aloud.

■ Have students who want to replace any words revise their paragraphs from Lesson 6 at home.

■ Have students share their revisions in groups, or have volunteers write their old and new sentences on the board.

What do you think?

page 118 **Giving feedback**

▦ Tell students that they are going to read each other's paragraphs and that they will need a sheet of paper for Exercise 2.

1

▦ Read the instructions for Exercises a–d aloud.

▦ Have students exchange their paragraphs with a partner and complete a–d. Walk around the classroom, helping students as necessary.

▦ Tell students to exchange books and review their partner's answers.

2

▦ Read the instructions for Exercise 2 aloud. Then call on a student to read the example letter.

▦ Have students write their letters to their partner individually.

▦ Walk around the classroom, helping students as necessary.

3

▦ Read the instructions for Exercise 3 aloud.

▦ Have students give their letters to their partner. Give them time to tell their partner the answer to the question in the letter.

▦ Have students revise their paragraphs based on the comments they receive and other ideas they have. They can complete their revisions either in class or at home.

▦ Have students turn in their revised paragraphs to you.

Make a card

page 119 **Just for fun**

▦ Bring or have students bring colored pencils or markers to class. They could also make their cards on a computer.

1

▦ Read the instructions for Exercises 1 and 1a aloud.

▦ Have students complete Exercise 1a individually.

▦ Read the instructions for Exercise 1b aloud. Explain vocabulary as necessary.

▦ Call on a student to read the poem on the card aloud.

▦ Have students complete the exercise individually.

▦ Walk around the classroom, helping students as necessary.

2

▦ Read the instructions for Exercises a–b aloud. Point out the example in the picture.

▦ Have students complete the exercise individually. If necessary, they can finish their cards at home.

3

▦ Read the instructions for Exercise 3 aloud.

▦ Set up a display table of all the cards or post them around the class, so that all the students have a chance to see the cards.

▦ Encourage students to send their cards to the appropriate person. Have students report the recipient's reactions to the class.